Introduction by U.S. Poet Laureate Kay Ryan

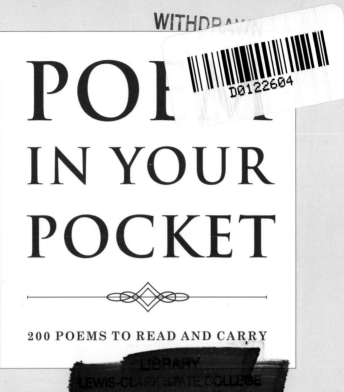

POE
IN YOUR
POCKET

200 POEMS TO READ AND CARRY

LIBRARY
LEWIS-CLARK STATE COLLEGE
LEWISTON, IDAHO

PUBLISHED IN CONJUNCTION WITH

THE ACADEMY OF AMERICAN POETS

Selected by Elaine Bleakney

ABRAMS IMAGE • NEW YORK

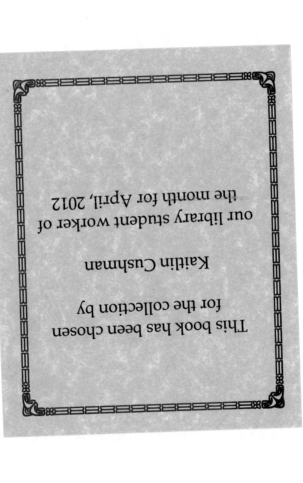

This book has been chosen
for the collection by

Kaitlin Cushman

our library student worker of
the month for April, 2012

Love & Rockets

CATCH

Big Boy came
Carrying a mermaid
On his shoulders
And the mermaid
Had her tail
Curved
Beneath his arm.

Being a fisher boy,
He'd found a fish
To carry—
Half fish,
Half girl
To marry.

BY LANGSTON HUGHES

TOE THE LINE WITH ME

We needed water & frozen water
for the party. I chose you to two-step

with but the downstairs chandelier
stayed still, its prisms prim.

Consider this: if sunfish
& ducks compete for the same bit

of bread, at any moment their mouths
might meet. That's how my mother

explained the Other, told me to hedge
my bets, furl wish-scrolls into

the topiary. Still I had questions
about Life & the Afterlife. You

looked in through the screen door.
I sat next to my ex.

BY MATTHEA HARVEY

KORE

As I was walking
    I came upon
chance walking
    the same road upon.

As I sat down
    by chance to move
later
    if and as I might,

light the wood was,
    light and green,
and what I saw
    before I had not seen.

It was a lady
    accompanied
by goat men
    leading her.

Her hair held earth.
    Her eyes were dark.
A double flute
    made her move.

'O love,
    where are you
leading
    me now?'

BY ROBERT CREELEY

THE GOOD-MORROW

I wonder, by my troth, what thou and I
Did, till we loved? were we not weaned till then?
But sucked on country pleasures, childishly?
Or snorted we in the Seven Sleepers' den?
'Twas so; but this, all pleasures fancies be.
If ever any beauty I did see,
Which I desired, and got, 'twas but a dream of thee.

And now good-morrow to our waking souls,
Which watch not one another out of fear;
For love, all love of other sights controls,
And makes one little room an everywhere.
Let sea-discoverers to new worlds have gone,
Let maps to others, worlds on worlds have shown,
Let us possess our world, each hath one, and is one.

My face in thine eye, thine in mine appears,
And true plain hearts do in the faces rest;
Where can we find two better hemispheres,
Without sharp North, without declining West?
Whatever dies was not mixed equally;
If our two loves be one, or, thou and I
Love so alike that none do slacken, none can die.

BY JOHN DONNE

From TWENTY-ONE LOVE POEMS

No one's fated or doomed to love anyone.
The accidents happen, we're not heroines,
they happen in our lives like car crashes,
books that change us, neighborhoods
we move into and come to love.
Tristan und Isolde is scarcely the story,
women at least should know the difference
between love and death. No poison cup,
no penance. Merely a notion that the tape-recorder
should have caught some ghost of us: that tape-recorder
not merely played but should have listened to us,
and could instruct those after us:
this we were, this is how we tried to love,
and these are the forces they had ranged against us,
and these are the forces we had ranged within us,
within us and against us, against us and within us.

BY ADRIENNE RICH

A Map of Love

Your face more than others' faces
Maps the half-remembered places
I have come to while I slept—
Continents a dream had kept
Secret from all waking folk
Till to your face I awoke,
And remembered then the shore,
And the dark interior.

By Donald Justice

THE HEART HAS NARROW BANKS

The Heart has narrow Banks
It measures like the Sea
In mighty – unremitting Bass
And Blue monotony

Till Hurricane bisect
And as itself discerns
It's insufficient Area
The Heart convulsive learns

That Calm is but a Wall
Of Unattempted Gauze
An instant's Push demolishes
A Questioning – dissolves.

BY EMILY DICKINSON

SONG

I hid my love when young while I
Coud'nt bear the buzzing of a flye
I hid my love to my despite
Till I could not bear to look at light
I dare not gaze upon her face
But left her memory in each place
Where ere I saw a wild flower lye
I kissed and bade my love good bye

I met her in the greenest dells
Where dew drops pearl the wood blue bells
The lost breeze kissed her bright blue eye
The Bee kissed and went singing bye
A sun beam found a passage there
A gold chain round her neck so fair
As secret as the wild bees song
She lay there all the summer long

I hid my love in field and town
Till e'en the breeze would knock me down
The Bees seemed singing ballads oe'r
The flyes buzz turned a Lions roar
And even silence found a tongue
To haunt me all the summer long
The Riddle nature could not prove
Was nothing else but secret love

BY JOHN CLARE

I LOVED YOU FIRST:
BUT AFTERWARDS YOUR LOVE

I loved you first: but afterwards your love
    Outsoaring mine, sang such a loftier song
As drowned the friendly cooings of my dove.
    Which owes the other most? My love was long,
    And yours one moment seemed to wax more strong;
I loved and guessed at you, you construed me
And loved me for what might or might not be –
    Nay, weights and measures do us both a wrong.
For verily love knows not 'mine' or 'thine;'
    With separate 'I' and 'thou' free love has done,
      For one is both and both are one in love:
Rich love knows nought of 'thine that is not mine;'
      Both have the strength and both the length thereof,
Both of us, of the love which makes us one.

BY CHRISTINA ROSSETTI

THE MORE LOVING ONE

Looking up at the stars, I know quite well
That, for all they care, I can go to hell,
But on earth indifference is the least
We have to dread from man or beast.

How should we like it were stars to burn
With a passion for us we could not return?
If equal affection cannot be,
Let the more loving one be me.

Admirer as I think I am
Of stars that do not give a damn,
I cannot, now I see them, say
I missed one terribly all day.

Were all stars to disappear or die,
I should learn to look at an empty sky
And feel its total dark sublime,
Though this might take me a little time.

By W.H. Auden

Summer in a Small Town

When the men leave me,
they leave me in a beautiful place.
It is always late summer.
When I think of them now,
I think of the place.
And being happy alone afterwards.
This time it's Clinton, New York.
I swim in the public pool
at six when the other people
have gone home.
The sky is grey, the air hot.
I walk back across the mown lawn
loving the smell and the houses
so completely it leaves my heart empty.

By Linda Gregg

COMMENT

Oh, life is a glorious cycle of song,
A medley of extemporanea;
And love is a thing that can never go wrong;
And I am Marie of Roumania.

BY DOROTHY PARKER

Juventius, honey-pot, I snatched from you while you were playing

---

Juventius, honey-pot, I snatched from you while you were playing
    a tiny kiss, sweeter than ambrosia's sweet.
But no way did I get it for free: an hour or longer,
    as I recall, you had me nailed on the cross
while I made abject apologies, yet all my weeping
    didn't abate your cruelty one jot.
Oh, the instant I'd done it you dabbed your lips with water,
    raised a soft hand and knuckled them clean, to ensure
no trace of my mouth should remain, as though expunging
    the filthy saliva of some pissed-on whore.
Since then, what's more, you've never quit making my love life
    a living hell, tormenting me every which way,
so that soon my poor kisslet turned from sweet to bitter,
    ambrosia no longer, but hellebore.
Well, since such is the penalty for my ill-starred passion,
    henceforth I will *never* snatch another kiss!

BY CATULLUS
TRANSLATED FROM THE LATIN BY PETER GREEN

Runaways Café II

For once, I hardly noticed what I ate
(salmon and broccoli and Saint-Véran).
My elbow twitched like jumping beans; sweat ran
into my shirtsleeves. Could I concentrate
on anything but your leg against mine
under the table? It was difficult,
but I impersonated an adult
looking at you, and knocking back the wine.
Now that we both want to know what we want,
now that we both want to know what we know,
it still behooves us to know what to do:
be circumspect, be generous, be brave,
be honest, be together, and behave.
At least I didn't get white sauce down my front.

By Marilyn Hacker

THE GUESTS

Our house was strewn with
people whom no one claimed
to know, people who had

been there for thirty years
or more. One might show
himself at dinner, cobwebbed

and thinner than the dead.
No one would speak of it,
unless the guest became

unpleasant, and then it was
in gestures, because our
voices were saved for something

better. Our dry lips flecked
with foam, our hammering hearts
out-waited our guests, and

now, at last, we are alone.

BY JAMES TATE

THE DREAM

O God, in the dream the terrible horse began
To paw at the air, and make for me with his blows.
Fear kept for thirty-five years poured through his mane,
And retribution equally old, or nearly, breathed through his nose.

Coward complete, I lay and wept on the ground
When some strong creature appeared, and leapt for the rein.
Another woman, as I lay half in a swound,
Leapt in the air, and clutched at the leather and chain.

Give him, she said, something of yours as a charm.
Throw him, she said, some poor thing you alone claim.
No, no, I cried, he hates me; he's out for harm,
And whether I yield or not, it is all the same.

But, like a lion in a legend, when I flung the glove
Pulled from my sweating, my cold right hand,
The terrible beast, that no one may understand,
Came to my side, and put down his head in love.

BY LOUISE BOGAN

THE FIST

The fist clenched round my heart
loosens a little, and I gasp
brightness; but it tightens
again. When have I ever not loved
the pain of love? But this has moved

past love to mania. This has the strong
clench of the madman, this is
gripping the ledge of unreason, before
plunging howling into the abyss.

Hold hard then, heart. This way at least you live.

BY DEREK WALCOTT

From TIME

Advice of good love: do not love
Women far away. Take one nearby,
As the right house takes stones
From its own place, stones that suffered in the cold
And glowed in the sun and were scorched.
Take the one with the golden wreath
Around her dark pupil, who knows something
About your death. You must love even
Among the ruins, like the honey
In Samson's devastated lion.

And advice of bad love: with the redundant
Love, left from the last one,
Make yourself a new wife, and with
What's left of her, make yourself
A new love,
Till nothing's left.

By Yehuda Amichai
translated from the Hebrew by Benjamin and Barbara Harshav

Paradise Motel

Millions were dead; everybody was innocent.
I stayed in my room. The President
Spoke of war as of a magic love potion.
My eyes were opened in astonishment.
In a mirror my face appeared to me
Like a twice-canceled postage stamp.

I lived well, but life was awful.
There were so many soldiers that day,
So many refugees crowding the roads.
Naturally, they all vanished
With a touch of the hand.
History licked the corners of its bloody mouth.

On the pay channel, a man and a woman
Were trading hungry kisses and tearing off
Each other's clothes while I looked on
With the sound off and the room dark
Except for the screen where the color
Had too much red in it, too much pink.

By Charles Simic

From THE REEF

So what is it, then, this being human,
except just being, here on the porch,
in the last square of sunlight,
dulled from some—
as it will seem much sooner than you think—
bearable blow.
You still can feel this last heat,
the softened and flowery breeze.
You can still hear the bird's static:
lovers pairing up all over town.

BY ELIZABETH ARNOLD

SINCE FEELING IS FIRST

since feeling is first
who pays any attention
to the syntax of things
will never wholly kiss you;

wholly to be a fool
while Spring is in the world

my blood approves,
and kisses are a better fate
than wisdom
lady i swear by all flowers. Don't cry
—the best gesture of my brain is less than
your eyelids' flutter which says

we are for each other: then
laugh, leaning back in my arms
for life's not a paragraph

And death i think is no parenthesis

BY E.E. CUMMINGS

From TO MARINA

Let's take a walk
Into the world
Where if our shoes get white
With snow, is it snow, Marina,
Is it snow or light?
Let's take a walk

Every detail is everything in its place (Aristotle). Literature is a cup
And we are the malted. The time is a glass. A June bug comes
And a carpenter spits on a plane, the flowers ruffle ear rings.
I am so dumb-looking. And you are so beautiful.

By Kenneth Koch

You're

Clownlike, happiest on your hands,
Feet to the stars, and moon-skulled,
Gilled like a fish. A common-sense
Thumbs-down on the dodo's mode.
Wrapped up in yourself like a spool,
Trawling your dark as owls do.
Mute as a turnip from the Fourth
Of July to All Fools' Day,
O high-riser, my little loaf.

Vague as fog and looked for like mail.
Farther off than Australia.
Bent-backed Atlas, our traveled prawn.
Snug as a bud and at home
Like a sprat in a pickle jug.
A creel of eels, all ripples.
Jumpy as a Mexican bean.
Right, like a well-done sum.
A clean slate, with your own face on.

By Sylvia Plath

MEDITATION ON FALLING

Sometimes to outwit love
I think I should throw my son
from my arms, or from the window,
or from the bridge where we watch the sun
light up the underbelly of cloud.
Hold me better, he says.

On falling, a shirt
fills with air—like a kite!
A hat flutters, a shoe
might be mistaken for a bird,
a necklace unfasten hook from eye
until the sky

in borrowed clothes
rises through the body
as in rage, or rapture.

BY CATHERINE BARNETT

A GOOD TIME

A good time to meet a new
Love is the same time
Good for placing a bomb.

At the juncture
Of season and season,
In blue absent-mindedness,
A slight confusion in the changing of the guards,
At the seam.

BY YEHUDA AMICHAI
TRANSLATED FROM THE HEBREW BY BENJAMIN AND BARBARA HARSHAV

Dwellings

FATHER'S BEDROOM

In my Father's bedroom:
blue threads as thin
as pen-writing on the bedspread,
blue dots on the curtains,
a blue kimono,
Chinese sandals with blue plush straps.
The broad-planked floor
had a sandpapered neatness.
The clear glass bed-lamp
with a white doily shade
was still raised a few
inches by resting on volume two
of Lafcadio Hearn's
Glimpses of Unfamiliar Japan.
Its warped olive cover
was punished like a rhinoceros hide.
In the flyleaf:
"Robbie from Mother."
Years later in the same hand:
"This book has had hard usage
on the Yangtze River, China.
It was left under an open
porthole in a storm."

BY ROBERT LOWELL

From THE GOD OF WINDOW-SCREENS AND HONEYSUCKLE

When I rock, the image in the double-paned glass
makes love to itself. I know the badly warped wood
that leaves long narrow pools on the drying deck means
I am lazy and the boards need to be replaced,
but god gets to assign meaning to the three cats
always replacing each other in my back yard
while my bare-chested, beach-ball-bellied neighbor sits
on his riding mower, his son on his lap, bored.
To plant beside the creek: one of the small hostas
split from its parent plant last fall, the cider jar full
of pennies, browntone photos of the ruined house,
a marker for the dog, nicknames of friends from school,
books I should read but never will, our old mattress,
the hundred desires I can name but not fulfill.

By H. L. Hix

BELL PEPPER

To find enough rooms for the gathering
The walls go on alone not waiting
For corners but thinking of sleeves
And how the wind fills them and the snow
Fills them and how cold it is without
Fires when there are not enough rooms.

BY JAMES MCMICHAEL

THE CABBAGE

You have rented an apartment.
You come to this enclosure with physical relief,
your heavy body climbing the stairs in the dark,
the hall bulb burned out, the landlord
of Greek extraction and possibly a fatalist.
In the apartment leaning against one wall,
your daughter's painting of a large frilled cabbage
against a dark sky with pinpoints of stars.
The eager vegetable, opening itself
as if to eat the air, or speak in cabbage
language of the meanings within meanings;
while the points of stars hide their massive
violence in the dark upper half of the painting.
You can live with this.

BY RUTH STONE

LOFT

I live in a bodiless loft,
no joists, beams,
or walls:

I huddle high,
arch my back against the stiff
fact of coming down:

my house admits to being
only above the level of most
perception:

I shudder and make do:
I don't look down.

By A. R. Ammons

TENT

Maybe it will fall away.
Maybe what is interesting will also be beautiful
although that is—
           that is:
not to look out or at, but into.
Come closer, so close
what you see can be seen as hindsight.
The form seems too simple.
The form seems an error of judgment.
As if one had jumped across a boundary
to find the missing gift, left
in the brute junk of wandering gangs.
This is another way of speaking about intention,
about the theater of gathering.

By Ann Lauterbach

From THE CELL

In the dark sky there
        are constellations, all of them
        erotic and they break open
        the streets
The streets exceed the house
On occasion the body exceeds
        the self
Everyday someone replaces someone and
        someone's mother is sad so
        as to exceed
The bed is a popular
        enclosure from which to depart
Outside the stars are stunning
        —touching
It is a question of
        scale
It is erotic when parts
        exceed their scale

BY LYN HEJINIAN

LEAVE-TAKING

Which of us will cry first, me or the house?
Soberly, placidly, off and on, glistening
over the old trails. How it holds over us

(here where marriage seems like a promise to keep
overflowing a small space) drifts on drifts
of web. Its spiders ravel the rafter shadows,

draw the walls down, intending—what? It only
knows, heavily, to hold us while we sleep.
While we sleep, the door warps in its frame.
Moss veins the front stoop, fretting the old stone.

(The different mosses.) Grass catches back from its falling
plumes, and holds in their parting, dew. You be

a statue. I'll be the little finished fountain
catching only the leaves, and rain.

BY JENNIFER CLARVOE

HOME IS SO SAD

Home is so sad. It stays as it was left,
Shaped to the comfort of the last to go
As if to win them back. Instead, bereft
Of anyone to please, it withers so,
Having no heart to put aside the theft

And turn again to what it started as,
A joyous shot at how things ought to be,
Long fallen wide. You can see how it was:
Look at the pictures and the cutlery.
The music in the piano stool. That vase.

BY PHILIP LARKIN

SLEEPING ON THE CEILING

It is so peaceful on the ceiling!
It is the Place de la Concorde.
The little crystal chandelier
is off, the fountain is in the dark.
Not a soul is in the park.

Below, where the wallpaper is peeling,
the Jardin des Plantes has locked its gates.
Those photographs are animals.
The mighty flowers and foliage rustle;
under the leaves the insects tunnel.

We must go under the wallpaper
to meet the insect-gladiator,
to battle with a net and trident,
and leave the fountain and the square.
But oh, that we could sleep up there...

BY ELIZABETH BISHOP

THE WINDOW

Position is where you
put it, where it is,
did you, for example, that

large tank there, silvered,
with the white church along–
side, lift

all that, to what
purpose? How
heavy the slow

world is with
everything put
in place. Some
man walks by, a
car beside him on
the dropped

road, a leaf of
yellow color is
going to

fall. It
all drops into
place. My

face is heavy
with the sight. I can
feel my eye breaking.

BY ROBERT CREELEY

CHILD ON TOP OF A GREENHOUSE

The wind billowing out the seat of my britches,
My feet crackling splinters of glass and dried putty,
The half-grown chrysanthemums staring up like accusers,
Up through the streaked glass, flashing with sunlight,
A few white clouds all rushing eastward,
A line of elms plunging and tossing like horses,
And everyone, everyone pointing up and shouting!

By Theodore Roethke

SHE HEARS THE STORM

There was a time in former years—
    While my roof-tree was his—
When I should have been distressed by fears
    At such a night as this!

I should have murmured anxiously,
    'The pricking rain strikes cold;
His road is bare of hedge or tree,
    And he is getting old.'

But now the fitful chimney-roar,
    The drone of Thorncombe trees,
The Froom in flood upon the moor,
    The mud of Mellstock Leaze,

The candle slanting sooty-wick'd,
    The thuds upon the thatch,
The eaves-drops on the window flicked,
    The clacking garden-hatch,

And what they mean to wayfarers,
    I scarcely heed or mind;
He has won that storm-tight roof of hers
    Which Earth grants all her kind.

BY THOMAS HARDY

ENTRANCE

No one in the house but the two, the one
on the way to death, the other
on the way to earth. Above, the white sky, not ready
to rain, below, lush, the mid-summer garden,
the thrush, or the young of the thrush,
or the seventeenth generation thrush.

Below, a door opens. No one moves about
but you, in the white chair, typing.

BY SASKIA HAMILTON

On Being a Householder

I lived inside a machine
or machines. Every time one
goes off another starts. Why
don't I go outside and sleep
on the ground. It is because
I'm scared of the open night
and stars looking down at me
as God's eyes, full of questions;
and when I do sleep out alone
I wake up soaking wet
with the dew-fall and am
being snuffed at by a female fox
who stinks from being skunked.
Also there are carrion insects
climbing my private parts. Therefore
I would find shelter in houses,
rented or owned. Anything that money
can build or buy is better than
the nothing of the sky at night,
the stars being the visible past.

By Alan Dugan

DESERT PLACES

Snow falling and night falling fast, oh, fast
In a field I looked into going past,
And the ground almost covered smooth in snow,
But a few weeds and stubble showing last.

The woods around it have it—it is theirs.
All animals are smothered in their lairs.
I am too absent-spirited to count;
The loneliness includes me unawares.

And lonely as it is that loneliness
Will be more lonely ere it will be less—
A blanker whiteness of benighted snow
With no expression, nothing to express.

They cannot scare me with their empty spaces
Between stars—on stars where no human race is.
I have it in me so much nearer home
To scare myself with my own desert places.

BY ROBERT FROST

YOU CANNOT PUT A FIRE OUT

You cannot put a Fire out –
A Thing that can ignite
Can go, itself, without a Fan –
Opon the slowest night –

You cannot fold a Flood –
And put it in a Drawer –
Because the Winds would find it out –
And tell your Cedar Floor –

BY EMILY DICKINSON

A Song in the Front Yard

I've stayed in the front yard all my life.
I want to peek at the back
Where it's rough and untended and hungry weed grows.
A girl gets sick of a rose.

I want to go in the back yard now
And maybe down the alley,
To where all the charity children play.
I want a good time today.

They do some wonderful things.
They have some wonderful fun.
My mother sneers, but I say it's fine
How they don't have to go in at quarter to nine.
My mother, she tells me that Johnnie Mae
Will grow up to be a bad woman.
That George'll be taken to Jail soon or late
(On account of last winter he sold our back gate).

But I say it's fine. Honest, I do.
And I'd like to be a bad woman, too,
And wear the brave stockings of night-black lace
And strut down the streets with paint on my face.

By Gwendolyn Brooks

Disillusionment of Ten O'Clock

The houses are haunted
By white night-gowns.
None are green,
Or purple with green rings,
Or green with yellow rings,
Or yellow with blue rings.
None of them are strange,
With socks of lace
And beaded ceintures.
People are not going
To dream of baboons and periwinkles.
Only, here and there, an old sailor,
Drunk and asleep in his boots,
Catches tigers
In red weather.

By Wallace Stevens

ANOTHER APRIL

The panes flash, tremble with your ghostly passage
Through them, an x-ray sheerness billowing, and I have risen
But cannot speak, remembering only that one was meant
To rise and not to speak. Young storm, this house is yours.
Let your eye darken, your rain come, the candle reeling
Deep in what still reflects control itself and me.
Daybreak's great gray rust-veined irises humble and proud
Along your path will have laid their foreheads in the dust.

By James Merrill

THE HOUSE

Do you still remember what the house was like?
The house—a pocket in a snowstorm's overcoat,
houses, low and bulging like Egyptian vowels.
Sheltered by green tongues of trees—
the most faithful was the linden, it shed
dry tears each fall.
Outmoded dresses dangled in the attic
like hanged men. Old letters flamed.
The old piano dozing in the parlor,
a hippo with black and yellow teeth.
On the wall a cross from a failed uprising
hung crookedly, and a photo
of a sad girl—a failed life.
The air smelled like vermouth,
bitter and sweet at once.
Houses, houses, where are you,
under what ocean, in what memory,
beneath the roof of what existence?
While the wind was opening windows, a deep blue
past sneaked into the rooms
and stifled the muslin curtains' breathing.
The fire was death's intended
and brought her bouquets of pale sparks.

BY ADAM ZAGAJEWSKI
TRANSLATED FROM THE POLISH BY CLARE CAVANAGH

THE LAKE ISLE OF INNISFREE

I will arise and go now, and go to Innisfree,
And a small cabin build there, of clay and wattles made;
Nine bean-rows will I have there, a hive for the honey-bee,
And live alone in the bee-loud glade.

And I shall have some peace there, for peace comes dropping slow,
Dropping from the veils of the morning to where the cricket sings;
There midnight's all a glimmer, and noon a purple glow,
And evening full of the linnet's wings.

I will arise and go now, for always night and day
I hear lake water lapping with low sounds by the shore;
While I stand on the roadway, or on the pavements grey,
I hear it in the deep heart's core.

BY WILLIAM BUTLER YEATS

What The Dog Perhaps Hears

If an inaudible whistle
blown between our lips
can send him home to us,
then silence is perhaps
the sound of spiders breathing
and roots mining the earth;
it may be asparagus heaving,
headfirst, into the light
and the long brown sound
of cracked cups, when it happens.

We would like to ask the dog
if there is a continuous whir
because the child in the house
keeps growing, if the snake
really stretches full length
without a click and the sun
breaks through clouds without
a decibel of effort,
whether in autumn, when the trees
dry up their wells, there isn't a shudder
too high for us to hear.

What is it like up there
above the shut-off level
of our simple ears?

For us there was no birth cry,
the newborn bird is suddenly here,
the egg broken, the nest alive,
and we heard nothing when the world changed.

By Lisel Mueller

NEST

I walked out, and the nest
was already there by the step. Woven basket
of a saint
sent back to life as a bird
who proceeded to make
a mess of things. Wind
right through it, and any eggs
long vanished. But in my hand it was
intricate pleasure, even the thorny reeds
softened in the weave. And the fading
leaf mold, hardly
itself anymore, merely a trick
of light, if light
can be tricked. Deep in a life
is another life. I walked out, the nest
already by the step.

BY MARIANNE BORUCH

OF MERE BEING

The palm at the end of the mind,
Beyond the last thought, rises
In the bronze decor,

A gold-feathered bird
Sings in the palm, without human meaning,
Without human feeling, a foreign song.

You know then that it is not the reason
That makes us happy or unhappy.
The bird sings. Its feathers shine.

The palm stands on the edge of space.
The wind moves slowly in the branches.
The bird's fire-fangled feathers dangle down.

BY WALLACE STEVENS

Eating & Drinking

CUTTING GREENS

curling them around
i hold their bodies in obscene embrace
thinking of everything but kinship.
collards and kale
strain against each strange other
away from my kissmaking hand and
the iron bedpot.
the pot is black.
the cutting board is black,
my hand,
and just for a minute
the greens roll black under the knife,
and the kitchen twists dark on its spine
and i taste in my natural appetite
the bond of live things everywhere.

BY LUCILLE CLIFTON

ALL THE SOUPS

All the soups I've made in my life—
slow-cooking easy broths, red thick
puréed blends. Churning it all up
alone in my kitchen, tasting,
covering, uncovering, remembering
spat-out carrots pinched between Mother's fingers
and pressed back into my mouth, Mother
wanting to get done with those meals, running
upstairs before Father comes home, Father
grubbing through drawers looking for pints,
both sisters up in the field getting plastered
and laid, me stuck in that chair,
locked behind a metal tray, not knowing
who's slamming the screen door so hard
that waves in my milk cup spill to my lap.
There's always a pot of soup on the stove.
I trace cats and houses on the damp kitchen wall,
waiting for anyone to come home,
waiting for one person
hungry enough to come home.

BY MARTHA RHODES

HONEY

I am three months out and six to go,
stuffing my plastic Superball body with the salt
& twang of crackers die-cut into the shapes of fish.
God forsakes me when I forsake him
but mostly he's much kinder, as is his duty:
I am radiant, people tell me, and have no hives,
except the swarm of gold bombs biting its way
into my sticky hollow. And I don't mean sex.
I am just a menagerie for bright orange creatures.
Even my dreams are godless (and full
of God): I dream I am guided
by an elderly couple in a dim farmhouse
to their morning radio and blackberry tea
and then given the combs which I snap
into my dry mouth where they fill and fill.
Never, upon awaking, have I been so empty
and wanted more a cracker. Never so
suffused with the weekly, with time
as another god passing through the many perfect
crypts and ambers I house beneath my skin.

BY ARIELLE GREENBERG

SELF-PORTRAIT AS A BEAR

Here is a fat animal, a bear
that is partly a dodo.
Ridiculous wings hang at his shoulders
as if they were collarbones
while he plods in the bad brickyards
at the edge of the city, smiling
and eating flowers. He eats them
because he loves them
because they are beautiful
because they love him.
It is eating flowers which makes him so fat.
He carries his huge stomach
over the gutters of damp leaves
in the parking lots in October,
but inside that paunch
he knows there are fields of lupine
and meadows of mustard and poppy.
He encloses sunshine.
Winds bend the flowers
in combers across the valley,
birds hang on the stiff wind,
at night there are showers, and the sun
lifts through a haze every morning
of the summer in the stomach.

BY DONALD HALL

LOST IN THE FOREST

I'd given up hope. Hadn't eaten in three
days. Resigned to being wolf meat...
when, unbelievably, I found myself in
a clearing. Two goats with bells
round their necks stared at me:
their pupils like coin slots
in piggy banks. I could have gotten
the truth out of those two,
if goats spoke. I saw leeks
and radishes planted in rows;
wash billowing on a clothesline...
and the innocuous-looking cottage
in the woods with its lapping tongue
of a welcome mat slurped me in.

In the kitchen, a woman so old her sex
is barely discernible pours a glass
of fraudulent milk. I'm so hungry
my hand shakes. But what is this liquid?
"Drink up, sweetheart," she says,
and as I wipe the white mustache
off with the back of my hand:
"Atta girl." Have I stumbled
into the clutches of St. Somebody?
Who can tell. "You'll find I prevail here
in my own little kingdom," she says as
she leads me upstairs—her bony grip
on my arm as a proclamation of ownership,
as though I've always been hers.

BY AMY GERSTLER

Devouring Time, blunt thou the lion's paws

Devouring Time, blunt thou the lion's paws,
And make the earth devour her own sweet brood;
Pluck the keen teeth from the fierce tiger's jaws,
And burn the long-lived phoenix in her blood;
Make glad and sorry seasons as thou fleet'st,
And do whate'er thou wilt, swift-footed Time,
To the wide world and all her fading sweets,
But I forbid thee one most heinous crime:
O, carve not with thy hours my love's fair brow,
Nor draw no lines there with thine antique pen;
Him in thy course untainted do allow
For beauty's pattern to succeeding men.
    Yet do thy worst, old Time: despite thy wrong,
    My love shall in my verse ever live young.

By William Shakespeare

KITCHEN SONG

The white bowls in the orderly
cupboards filled with nothing.

The sound
of applause in running water.
All those who've drowned in oceans, all
who've drowned in pools, in ponds, the small
family together in the car hit head on. The pantry

full of lilies, the lobsters scratching to get out of the pot, and
    God

being pulled across the heavens
in a burning car.

The recipes
like confessions.
The confessions like songs.
The sun. The bomb. The white

bowls in the orderly
cupboards filled with blood. *I wanted*

something simple, and domestic. A kitchen song.

They were just driving along. Dad
turned the radio off, and Mom
turned it back on.

By Laura Kasischke

FREEZER

Where eyes of round have forgotten
the quick knife that made them,
how the butcher stared against the light
as he leaned in his smeary apron
separating the parts of a carcass
that yet knew something of what he did—
that pain is gone. Where pale ears of corn
have forgotten how the wind used to dance
in their stalks, how bees would hum
in the close indigo. Where okra has frozen
in green fingers, which point
to the hearts of calves, grazing
in the rising grass of high summer,
not noticing that the egrets have begun
to leave, any more than they noticed
that their mothers had disappeared,
or that the moon was slow orange all week.
Only the freezer knows the truth—the end
of all such stories, after the ends
our mothers tell us as they smile on our beds
before they turn out the lights.
The last home of animals and gardens.
The dark. The cold. The waiting to be eaten.

BY LOLA HASKINS

RED MEANS

Red be-ings
whose history is
Adam's apple
Guyaba at the
entrance
To the cave
Which Lucifer
Entered to
Terminate with
darkness
Taking that ride
up the throat
Finding the stove
of the kitchen
Where someone
Had been up earlier
Cooking Red Beans

BY VICTOR HERNÁNDEZ CRUZ

AVOCADO

The Dharma is like an Avocado!
Some parts so ripe you can't believe it,
But it's good.
And other places hard and green
Without much flavor,
Pleasing those who like their eggs well-cooked.

And the skin is thin,
The great big round seed
In the middle,
Is your own Original Nature—
Pure and smooth,
Almost nobody ever splits it open
Or ever tries to see
If it will grow.

Hard and slippery,
It looks like
You should plant it—but then
It shoots out thru the
       fingers—
gets away.

BY GARY SNYDER

WATERMELONS

Green Buddhas
On the fruit stand.
We eat the smile
And spit out the teeth.

BY CHARLES SIMIC

WATERMELON

Apple

Apple plum, carpet steak, seed clam, colored wine, calm seen, cold cream, best shake, potato, potato and no no gold work with pet, a green seen is called bake and change sweet is bready, a little piece a little piece please.

A little piece please. Cane again to the presupposed and ready eucalyptus tree, count out sherry and ripe plates and little corners of a kind of ham. This is use.

By Gertrude Stein

SPAGHETTI

Not infrequently destroyed as bits of paper
of no value by the women in my family,
namely Ida, Libby, and the maid Thelma,
my drawings were gone by the time I was eleven
and so I turned to music and led orchestras
walking through the woods, and Saturday nights
we feasted on macaroni, tomato soup and falso
cheese cooked at three hundred fifty degrees
which I called spaghetti until I was 21
and loved our nights there, Thelma, Libby, and Ida,
fat as I was then, fat and near-sighted
and given over to art, such as I saw it,
though smothered somewhat by the three of them;
and it would be five years of breaking loose,
reading Kropotkin first, then reading Keats,
and standing on my head and singing by which
I developed the longing though I never
turned against that spaghetti, I was always
loyal to one thing, you could almost measure
my stubbornness and my wildness by that loyalty.

By Gerald Stern

BITTER-SWEET

Ah my dear angry Lord,
Since those dost love, yet strike;
Cast down, yet help afford;
Sure I will do the like.

I will complain, yet praise;
I will bewail, approve:
And all my sour-sweet days
I will lament, and love.

BY GEORGE HERBERT

THE AUTHOR LOVING THESE HOMELY MEATS SPECIALLY, VIZ.: CREAM, PANCAKES, BUTTERED PIPPIN-PIES (LAUGH, GOOD PEOPLE) AND TOBACCO; WRIT TO THAT WORTHY AND VIRTUOUS GENTLEWOMAN, WHOM HE CALLETH MISTRESS, AS FOLLOWETH

If there were, oh! an Hellespont of cream
Between us, milk-white mistress, I would swim
To you, to show to both my love's extreme,
Leander-like,—yea! dive from brim to brim.
But met I with a buttered pippin-pie
Floating upon 't, that would I make my boat
To waft me to you without jeopardy,
Though sea-sick I might be while it did float.
Yet if a storm should rise, by night or day,
Of sugar-snows and hail of caraways,
Then, if I found a pancake in my way,
It like a plank should bring me to your kays;
   Which having found, if they tobacco kept,
    The smoke should dry me well before I slept.

BY JOHN DAVIES

From LEAP

this is the second shower
I've taken today I didn't
need to take this one
all I did today was
wake up and watch TV

at one point I walked
to the grocery store and
bought a pound of strawberries
for 99 cents they weren't
too tart if my body

is found I want them
to pack it with strawberries
I want my casket lined
with strawberries I want them
to bulldoze strawberries over me

BY JON WOODWARD

I Wake and Feel the Fell of Dark

I wake and feel the fell of dark, not day.
What hours, O what black hoürs we have spent
This night! what sights you, heart, saw; ways you went!
And more must, in yet longer light's delay.

With witness I speak this. But where I say
Hours I mean years, mean life. And my lament
Is cries countless, cries like dead letters sent
To dearest him that lives alas! away.

I am gall, I am heartburn. God's most deep decree
Bitter would have me taste: my taste was me;
Bones built in me, flesh filled, blood brimmed the curse.

Selfyeast of spirit a dull dough sours. I see
The lost are like this, and their scourge to be
As I am mine, their sweating selves; but worse.

By Gerard Manley Hopkins

From MODERN LOVE

At dinner, she is hostess, I am host.
Went the feast ever cheerfuller? She keeps
The Topic over intellectual deeps
In buoyancy afloat. They see no ghost.
With sparkling surface-eyes we ply the ball:
It is in truth a most contagious game:
HIDING THE SKELETON, shall be its name.
Such play as this the devils might appal!
But here's the greater wonder; in that we,
Enamoured of an acting nought can tire,
Each other, like true hypocrites, admire;
Warm-lighted looks, Love's ephemeræ,
Shoot gaily o'er the dishes and the wine.
We waken envy of our happy lot.
Fast, sweet, and golden, shows the marriage-knot.
Dear guests, you now have seen Love's corpse-light shine.

BY GEORGE MEREDITH

A Drinking Song

Wine comes in at the mouth
And love comes in at the eye;
That's all we shall know for truth
Before we grow old and die.
I lift the glass to my mouth,
I look at you, and I sigh.

By William Butler Yeats

THE THIRTIES

The thirties
I don't exist yet
Grass grows
A girl eats strawberry ice cream
Someone listens to Schumann
(mad, ruined
Schumann)
I don't exist yet
How fortunate
I can hear everything

BY ADAM ZAGAJEWSKI
TRANSLATED FROM THE POLISH BY CLARE CAVANAGH

TOMATO

My friend Amy has a jones for pregnant women,
wants to fan their flushed faces, pull out chairs for them,
carry parasols above them in strong sunlight,
fix figs with mascarpone for the calcium and iron.

I long to be the rosy, pregnant woman people flock to,
hear other women's chuttering wisdom, tales:
a sister whose teeth fell out from too many babies,
milk that spurts across the room at any cry.
Her hair went curly. Her hair went straight.
Her face erupted in red sprinkles.
How are you eating? What are you dreaming?
Dream of strawberries, the baby will have rashes.

And then one night I dream of Susan Sarandon.
She's a radiant red tomato in a straw sun hat,
digging in the rows of her organic garden patch,
a million months pregnant,

and her lover is feeding her chocolate, square by square.

BY ELIZABETH ALEXANDER

STYROFOAM CUP

thou still unravished   thou

thou,   thou bride

thou unstill,

thou unravished   unbride

unthou unbride

BY BRENDA HILLMAN

A GLASS OF WATER

Here is a glass of water from my well.
It tastes of rock and root and earth and rain;
It is the best I have, my only spell,
And it is cold, and better than champagne.
Perhaps someone will pass this house one day
To drink, and be restored, and go his way,
Someone in dark confusion as I was
When I drank down cold water in a glass,
Drank a transparent health to keep me sane,
After the bitter mood had gone again.

BY MAY SARTON

GOING OFF THE DEEP END
INTO CONFECTIONERY

We're the anemones guarding
the gates of infinity,

the boats squidding in the bay.
In the flooded fish market,

dead fish, live fish—who took you
to the Tuileries for a rose-

scented swim? Turn the world
& the page is pink.

Frond-fond & pond-proud,
we sugar the obstacle dark.

BY MATTHEA HARVEY

Ciao Bella Chocolate Sorbet

has a dense
chewy

water-to-chocolate
ratio

as if a whole
devil's food cake

were dissolved
in each scoop.

Delivers Elvis-like
indulgence

for only 120 calories.
By the last spoonful,

your whole nervous system
and aura

will be permeated
by the ancient Mayan God.

You will see
through the eyes of Chocolate.

By Elaine Equi

Friends & Ghosts

I Saw in Louisiana
a Live-Oak Growing

I saw in Louisiana a live-oak growing,
All alone stood it and the moss hung down from the branches,
Without any companion it grew there uttering joyous leaves of
    dark green,
And its look, rude, unbending, lusty, made me think of myself,
But I wonder'd how it could utter joyous leaves standing alone
    there without its friend near, for I knew I could not,
And I broke off a twig with a certain number of leaves upon it,
    and twined around it a little moss,
And brought it away, and I have placed it in sight in my room,
It is not needed to remind me as of my own dear friends,
(For I believe lately I think of little else than of them,)
Yet it remains to me a curious token, it makes me think of
    manly love;
For all that, and though the live-oak glistens there in
    Louisiana solitary in a wide flat space,
Uttering joyous leaves all its life without a friend a lover near,
I know very well I could not.

By Walt Whitman

ANIMALS

Have you forgotten what we were like then
when we were still first rate
and the day came fat with an apple in its mouth

it's no use worrying about Time
but we did have a few tricks up our sleeves
and turned some sharp corners

the whole pasture looked like our meal
we didn't need speedometers
we could manage cocktails out of ice and water

I wouldn't want to be faster
or greener than now if you were with me O you
were the best of all my days

BY FRANK O'HARA

LETTER
for Richard Howard

Men are running across a field,
pens fall from their pockets.
People out walking will pick them up.
It is one of the ways letters are written.

How things fall to others!
The self no longer belonging to me, but asleep
in a stranger's shadow, now clothing
the stranger, now leading him off.

It is noon as I write to you.
Someone's life has come into my hands.
The sun whitens the buildings.
It is all I have. I give it all to you. Yours,

BY MARK STRAND

SADIE AND MAUD

Maud went to college.
Sadie stayed at home.
Sadie scraped life
With a fine-tooth comb.

She didn't leave a tangle in.
Her comb found every strand.
Sadie was one of the livingest chits
In all the land.

Sadie bore two babies
Under her maiden name.
Maud and Ma and Papa
Nearly died of shame.

When Sadie said her last so-long
Her girls struck out from home.
(Sadie had left as heritage
Her fine-tooth comb.)

Maud, who went to college,
Is a thin brown mouse.
She is living all alone
In this old house.

BY GWENDOLYN BROOKS

MARGARET AND DUSTY

Margaret wrote a letter
sealed it with her finger
put it in her pocket
for the Dusty Baker

Dusty was his bat
Dusty was his moustache
Dusty was Margaret's pocket
They both got all dusty

If I had a flower
If I had a trinket of gold
      & silver & lapis
If I had a medal & a trophy
      & a fullup sticker album
I'd rather be all dusty
Like those two friends of mine.

BY ALICE NOTLEY

THE REASSURANCE

About ten days or so
After we saw you dead
You came back in a dream.
I'm all right now you said.

And it was you, although
You were fleshed out again:
You hugged us all round them,
And gave your welcoming beam.

How like you to be kind,
Seeking to reassure.
And, yes, how like my mind
To make itself secure.

BY THOM GUNN

WHY HE WAS THERE

Much as he left it when he went from us
Here was the room again where he had been
So long that something of him should be seen,
Or felt—and so it was. Incredulous,

I turned about, loath to be greeted thus,
And there he was in his old chair, serene
As ever, and as laconic and as lean
As when he lived, and as cadaverous.

Calm as he was of old when we were young,
He sat there gazing at the pallid flame
Before him. "And how far will this go on?"
I thought. He felt the failure of my tongue,
And smiled: "I was not here until you came;
And I shall not be here when you are gone."

BY EDWIN ARLINGTON ROBINSON

ARE FRIENDS DELIGHT OR PAIN?

Are Friends Delight or Pain?
Could Bounty but remain
Riches were good –

But if they only stay
Ampler to fly away
Riches are sad.

BY EMILY DICKINSON

Consider a Move

The steady time of being unknown,
in solitude, without friends,
is not a steadiness that sustains.
I hear your voice waver on the phone:

Haven't talked to anyone for days.
I drive around, I sit in parking lots.
The voice zeroes through my ear, and waits.
What should I say? There are ways

to meet people you will want to love?
I know of none. You come out stronger
having gone through this? I no longer
believe that, if I once did. Consider a move,

a change, a job, a new place to live,
some place you'd like to be. *That's not it*,
you say. Now time curves back. We almost touch.
Then what is? I ask. What is?

By Michael Ryan

BEES
for Sandra McPherson

A man whose arms and shoulders
and hands and face and ears are covered with bees
says, *I've never known such pain.*
Another man comes over
with bees all over his hands—
only bees can get the other bees off.
The first man says again,
I've never known such pain.
The second man's bees begin to pluck
the first grave yellow bees off, one by one.

BY JEAN VALENTINE

THE WOUND

The shock comes slowly
as an afterthought.

First you hear the words
and they are like all other words,

ordinary, breathing out of lips,
moving toward you in a straight line.

Later they shatter
and rearrange themselves. They spell

something else hidden in the muscles
of the face, something the throat wanted to say.

Decoded, the message etches itself in acid
so every syllable becomes a sore.

The shock blooms into a carbuncle.
The body bends to accommodate it.

A special scarf has to be worn to conceal it.
It is now the size of a head.

The next time you look,
it has grown two eyes and a mouth.

It is difficult to know which to use.
Now you are seeing everything twice.

After a while it becomes an old friend.
It reminds you every day of how it came to be.

BY RUTH STONE

From STANZAS IN MEDITATION

I think very well of Susan but I do not know her name
I think very well of Ellen but which is not the same
I think very well of Paul I tell him not to do so
I think very well of Francis Charles but do I do so
I think very well of Thomas but I do not not do so
I think very well of not very well of William
I think very well of any very well of him
I think very well of him.
It is remarkable how quickly they learn
But if they learn and it is very remarkable how quickly they learn
It makes not only but by and by
And they can not only be not here
But not there
Which after all makes no difference
After all this does not make any does not make any difference
I add added it to it.
I could rather be rather be here.

BY GERTRUDE STEIN

THAT SURE IS MY LITTLE DOG

Yes, indeed, that is my house that I am carrying around
on my back like a bullet-proof shell and yes, that sure is
my little dog walking a hard road in hard boots. And
just wait until you see my girl, chomping on the chains
of fate with her mouth full of jagged steel. She's damn
ready and so am I. What else did you expect from the
brainiacs of my generation? The survivors, the nonbelievers,
the oddball-outs with the Cuban Missile Crisis still
sizzling in our blood? Don't tell me that you bought
our act, just because our worried parents (and believe me,
we're nothing like them) taught us how to dress for work
and to speak as if we cared about our education. And
I guess the music fooled you: you thought we'd keep
the party going even to the edge of the abyss. Well,
too bad. It's all yours now. Good luck on the ramparts.
What you want to watch for is when the sky shakes
itself free of kites and flies away. Have a nice day.

BY ELEANOR LERMAN

WHITE DOG

First snow—I release her into it—
I know, released, she won't come back.
This is different from letting what,

already, we count as lost go. It is nothing
like that. Also, it is not like wanting to learn what
losing a thing we love feels like. Oh yes:

I love her.
Released, she seems for a moment as if
some part of me that, almost,

I wouldn't mind
understanding better, is that
not love? She seems a part of me,

and then she seems entirely like what she is:
a white dog,
less white suddenly, against the snow,

who won't come back. I know that; and, knowing it,
I release her. It's as if I release her
because I know.

BY CARL PHILLIPS

DEFINITION OF STRANGER

Person not a member
of a group. A visitor,
guest, or the breast
that brushes your arm
on the subway. Person
with whom you've had
no acquaintance but who's taken
your rocking chair
from the curbside
and curls up in it
and closes her eyes.
Person in line
behind you now, waiting
for a glass of water,
or of whiskey, of elixir.
Person logging online
at the same second
from the Home Depot in Lima.
Or in search of the Dalai Lama.
Person not privy or party
to a decision, edict, et cetera,
but who's eaten
from the same fork
at the pizzeria
and kissed your wilder sister
on New Year's. Person assigned
to feed the tiger at the zoo
where you slipped your hand
                                    once
into the palm
of somebody else's father.

BY IDRA NOVEY

THESE STRANGERS,
IN A FOREIGN WORLD

These Strangers, in a foreign World,
Protection asked of me –
Befriend them, lest yourself in Heaven
Be found a Refugee –

BY EMILY DICKINSON

People Getting Divorced

People getting divorced
      riding around with their clothes in the car
  and wondering what happened
        to everyone and everything
          including their other
                pair of shoes
    And if you spy one
      then who knows what happened
                to the other one
            with tongue alack
  and years later not even knowing
        if the other ever
          found a mate
          without splitting the seams
          or remained intact
              unlaced
  and the sole
      ah the soul
          a curious conception
 hanging on somehow
        to walk again
           in the free air
      once the heel
          has been replaced

By Lawrence Ferlinghetti

Song

My heart, my dove, my snail, my sail, my
  milktooth, shadow, sparrow, fingernail,
    flower-cat and blossom-hedge, mandrake

root now put to bed, moonshell, sea-swell,
  manatee, emerald shining back at me,
    nutmeg, quince, tea leaf and bone, zither,

cymbal, xylophone; paper, scissors, then
  there's stone—Who doesn't come through the door
    to get home?

By Cynthia Zarin

POEM

You called, you're on the train, on Sunday,
I have just taken a shower and await
you. Clouds are slipping in off the ocean,
but the room is gently lit by the green
shirt you gave me. I have been practicing
a new way to say hello and it is fantastic.
You were so sad: goodbye. I was so sad.
All the shops were closed but the sky
was high and blue. I tried to walk it off
but I must have walked in the wrong direction.

BY MATTHEW ROHRER

THE SHAMPOO

The still explosions on the rocks,
the lichens, grow
by spreading, gray, concentric shocks.
They have arranged
to meet the rings around the moon, although
within our memories they have not changed.

And since the heavens will attend
as long on us,
you've been, dear friend,
precipitate and pragmatical;
and look what happens. For Time is
nothing if not amenable.

The shooting stars in your black hair
in bright formation
are flocking where,
so straight, so soon?
—Come, let me wash it in this big tin basin,
battered and shiny like the moon.

BY ELIZABETH BISHOP

THE POOL

Are you alive?
I touch you.
You quiver like a sea-fish.
I cover you with my net.
What are you—banded one?

By H.D.

MAN OF WAR

After there were no women, men, and children,

from the somber deeps horseshoe crabs crawled up on somber shores:

Man-of-Wars' blue sails drifted downwind

and blue filaments of some biblical cloak

floated below: the stinging filaments.

The cored of bone and rock-headed came near:

clouds made wandering shadows:

sea and grasses mingled::

There was no hell after all

but a lull before it began over::

flesh lying alone: then mating: a little spray of soul:

and the grace of waves, of stars, and remotest isles.

BY CAROL FROST

WINTER

I don't know what to say to you, neighbor,
as you shovel snow from your part of our street
neat in your Greek black. I've waited for
chance to find words; now, by chance, we meet.

We took our boys to the same kindergarten,
thirteen years ago when our husbands went.
Both boys hated school, dropped out feral, dropped in
to separate troubles. You shift snow fast, back bent,
but your boy killed himself, six days dead.

My boy washed your wall when the police were done.
He says, "We weren't friends?" and shakes his head,
"I told him it was great he had that gun,"
and shakes. I shake, close to you, close to you.
You have a path to clear, and so you do.

BY MARIE PONSOT

THE UNDERWORLD

The exhausted dead lean on silvery pillars.
The frilly scent of pear blossoms mixes
easily with the heavier smells of fried food
that hang jagged, spiking the air
like invisible stalactites. There *is*
a river: Women who murdered their husbands
with hairpins study Plato daily.
Saints are encouraged to complain at length,
to dress better, sweeten their anxious,
famished breath by gumming mint leaves.
Horizons broaden. The pear blossoms wither
and drop off. Hard little knobs of fruit swell
underneath. Harmless, noiseless swordplay
takes place. There are plenty of figs
to use in making nice sticky brown jam.
Pigs squeal throughout. Bedrooms are decorated
in either the fierce heraldic hues
of an ancient age or all nineteen
shades of white identified by the Eskimos,
a color scheme even the recalcitrant dead,
who refuse to rise, find surprisingly reviving.

BY AMY GERSTLER

MY SAD CAPTAINS

One by one they appear in
the darkness: a few friends, and
a few with historical
names. How late they start to shine!
but before they fade they stand
perfectly embodied, all

the past lapping them like a
cloak of chaos. They were men
who, I thought, lived only to
renew the wasteful force they
spent with each hot convulsion.
They remind me, distant now.

True, they are not at rest yet,
but now that they are indeed
apart, winnowed from failures,
they withdraw to an orbit
and turn with disinterested
hard energy, like the stars.

BY THOM GUNN

Myself I Speak & Spell

BEGINNING MY STUDIES

Beginning my studies, the first step pleas'd me so much,
The mere fact, consciousness—these forms—the power of motion,
The least insect or animal—the senses—eyesight;
The first step, I say, aw'd me and pleas'd me so much,
I have never gone, and never wish'd to go, any farther,
But stop and loiter all my life, to sing it in extatic songs.

BY WALT WHITMAN

OLYMPIA

Tired, hungry, hot, I climbed the steep slope

to town, a sultry, watery place, crawling with insects

and birds.

      In the semidarkness of the mountain,

small things loomed large: a donkey urinating on a palm;

a salt-and-saliva-stained boy riding on his mother's back;

a shy roaming black Adam. I was walking on an edge.

The moments fused into one crystalline rock,

like ice in a champagne bucket. Time was plunging forward,

like dolphins scissoring open water or like me,

following Jenny's flippers down to see the coral reef,

where the color of sand, sea and sky merged,

and it was as if that was all God wanted:

not a wife, a house or a position,

but a self, like a needle, pushing in a vein.

BY HENRI COLE

Afternoon on a Hill

I will be the gladdest thing
   Under the sun!
I will touch a hundred flowers
And not pick one.

I will look at cliffs and clouds
   With quiet eyes,
Watch the wind bow down the grass,
   And the grass rise.

And when lights begin to show
   Up from the town,
I will mark which must be mine,
   And then start down!

By Edna St. Vincent Millay

As kingfishers catch fire, dragonflies draw flame

As kingfishers catch fire, dragonflies draw flame;
As tumbled over rim in roundy wells
Stones ring; like each tucked string tells, each hung bell's
Bow swung finds tongue to fling out broad its name;
Each mortal thing does one thing and the same:
Deals out that being indoors each one dwells;
Selves—goes itself; *myself* it speaks and spells,
Crying *What I do is me: for that I came.*

I say more: the just man justices;
Keeps grace: that keeps all his goings graces;
Acts in God's eye what in God's eye he is—
Christ—for Christ plays in ten thousand places,
Lovely in limbs, and lovely in eyes not his
To the Father through the features of men's faces.

By Gerard Manley Hopkins

ECHO'S SONG

Slow, slow, fresh fount, keep time with my salt tears;
    Yet slower, yet; O faintly gentle springs:
List to the heavy part the music bears,
    Woe weeps out her division, when she sings.
        Droop herbs and flowers;
        Fall grief in showers;
        Our beauties are not ours;
           O, I could still,
Like melting snow upon some craggy hill,
        Drop, drop, drop, drop,
Since nature's pride is, now, a withered daffodil.

By Ben Jonson

No Better Than
a "Withered Daffodil"

Ben Jonson said he was? "O I could still
Like melting snow upon some craggy hill,
         Drop, drop, drop, drop."

I too until I saw that French brocade
blaze green as though some lizard in the shade
         became exact—

set off by replicas of violet—
like Sidney, leaning in his striped jacket
         against a lime—

a work of art. And I too seemed to be
an insouciant rester by a tree—
         no daffodil.

By Marianne Moore

TENDERNESS AND ROT

Tenderness and rot
share a border.
And rot is an
aggressive neighbor
whose iridescence
keeps creeping over.

No lessons
can be drawn
from this however.

One is not
two countries.
One is not meat
corrupting.

It is important
to stay sweet
and loving.

BY KAY RYAN

WARNING

Lovers of hunting,
and beginners seeking your prey:
Don't aim your rifles
at my happiness,
which isn't worth
the price of the bullet
(you'd waste on it).
What seems to you
so nimble and fine,
like a fawn,
and flees
every which way,
like a partridge,
isn't happiness.
Trust me:
My happiness bears
no relation to happiness.

BY TAHA MUHAMMAD ALI
TRANSLATED FROM THE ARABIC BY PETER COLE

THE BEARHUG

It's not as if I'm intending on spending the rest of my life
        doing this:
besuited, rebooted, filing to work, this poem a fishbone in
        my briefcase.
The scaffolding clinging to St Paul's is less urban ivy than
        skin, peeling off.

A singular sprinkler shaking his head spits at the newsprint
        of birdshit.
It's going unread: Gooseberry Poptarts, stale wheaten
        bread, Nutella and toothpaste.
An open-armed crane turns to embrace the aeroplanes
        passing above.

I hadn't the foggiest notion. Imagine: me, munching
        cardboard and rubbish,
but that's just what they meant when they said, *Come in,
        you're dead-beat,*
take the weight off your paws, you're a big weary grizzly
        with a hook through his mouth,

here, have some of this love.

By Nick Laird

SAMURAI SONG

When I had no roof I made
Audacity my roof. When I had
No supper my eyes dined.

When I had no eyes I listened.
When I had no ears I thought.
When I had no thought I waited.

When I had no father I made
Care my father. When I had
No mother I embraced order.

When I had no friend I made
Quiet my friend. When I had no
Enemy I opposed my body.

When I had no temple I made
My voice my temple. I have
No priest, my tongue is my choir.

When I have no means fortune
Is my means. When I have
Nothing, death will be my fortune.

Need is my tactic, detachment
Is my strategy. When I had
No lover I courted my sleep.

BY ROBERT PINSKY

AN OLD CRACKED TUNE

My name is Solomon Levi,
the desert is my home,
my mother's breast was thorny,
and father I had none.

The sands whispered, *Be separate*,
the stones taught me, *Be hard*.
I dance, for the joy of surviving,
on the edge of the road.

BY STANLEY KUNITZ

REMORA

This life is deep and dense
Beyond all seeing, yet one sees, in spite
Of being littler, a degree or two
Further than those one is attracted to.

Pea-brained, myopic, often brutal,
When chosen they have no defense—
A sucking sore there on the belly's pewter—
And where two go could be one's finer sense.

Who now descends from a machine
Plumed with bubbles, death in his right hand?
Lunge, numbskull! One, two, three worlds boil.
Thanks for the lift. There are other fish in the sea.

Still on occasion as by oversight
One lets be taken clinging fast
In heavenly sunshine to the corpse a slight
Tormented self, live, dapper, black-and-white.

BY JAMES MERRILL

HULA

While I was writing my poem
Patty was doing the crossword puzzle
Hula was the word she got
Plus an all-expense paid trip to Hawaii

Now I live here all alone
A short fat figure made of grey stone
And as the flowers go past my door
I see their shadows move across the floor

The doughnut sings its pretty song
And so does sing the tellyvision
The purple martin flies for fun
The purple martin flies for fun

The purple martin flies for fun
Around the ego's solar system
Which hangs there like an illustration
That we are truly a great nation

BY RON PADGETT

MR. T—

A man made of scrap muscle & the steam
engine's imagination, white feathers
flapping in each lobe for the skull's migration,
should the need arise. Sometimes drugged
& duffled (by white men) in a cockpit
bound for the next adventure. And liable
to crush a fool's face like newsprint; headlines
of Hollywood blood and wincing. Half Step 'N Fetchit,
half John Henry. What were we, the skinny B-boys,
to learn from him? How to hulk through Chicago
in a hedgerow afro, an ox-grunt kicking dust
behind the teeth; those eighteen glammering
gold chains around the throat of pity,
that fat hollow medallion like the sun on a leash—

BY TERRANCE HAYES

FAME:
MY VERSION

Somehow in the seeking
I confused *fame* with *frame*:
I pressed my face to picture windows
of houses I couldn't afford to live in,
I folded myself into the dumbwaiters
of old ornate hotels.
None of this was picked up by the press.
I spent my mornings constructing
model houses from toothpicks and glue.
A lonely labor, though some
who had gone before me
had achieved immortality
through a similar attention to form.
While some men fingerprinted me
no charges were ever filed,
my grim profile never graced a post office wall.
The only public estimates had me
as rumor, and my public had shrunk
to five or six individuals
since I'd ceased to speak with the voice
I was born to. In the sole home movie
that survived my childhood
I appear in one exposure—
there I am, blink, I'm gone.
A million hands clapping
while I flamed out still nameless.

BY COURTNEY QUEENEY

WHAT BEE DID

Bee not only buzzed.
When swatted at, Bee deviled,
Bee smirched. And when fuddled,
like many of us, Bee labored, Bee reaved.
He behaved as well as any Bee can have.

Bee never lied. Bee never lated.
And despite the fact Bee took, Bee also stowed.
In love, Bee seiged. Bee seeched.
Bee moaned, Bee sighed himself,
Bee gat with his Beloved.

And because Bee tokened summer
(the one season we all, like Bee, must lieve)
Bee also dazzled.

BY JULIE LARIOS

WIRING HOME

Lest the wolves loose their whistles
and shopkeepers inquire,

keep moving; though your knees flush
red as two chapped apples,

keep moving, head up,
past the beggar's cold cup,

past fires banked under chestnuts
and the trumpeting kiosk's

tales of odyssey and heartbreak
until, turning a corner, you stand

staring: ambushed
by a window of canaries

bright as a thousand
golden narcissi.

BY RITA DOVE

THE WIND STOPPED
FOR A MOMENT

The wind stopped for a moment at the end of autumn and twilight; a woman called across the yards to her young son, toward the blueing trees, tired faces of workers who glimpsed the moon beginning. Some things are only bright in the darkness. Some people never have their time. They feel like certain birds and fish designed especially to go through.

By Killarney Clary

DUSK

spider on the cold expanse
of glass, three stories high
rests intently
and so purely alone.

I'm not like that!

BY RAE ARMANTROUT

Wind in a Box

This ink. This name. This blood. This blunder.
This blood. This loss. This lonesome wind. This canyon.
This / twin / swiftly / paddling / shadow blooming
an inch above the carpet—. This cry. This mud.
This shudder. This is where I stood: by the bed,
by the door, by the window, in the night / in the night.
How deep, how often / must a woman be touched?
How deep, how often have I been touched?
On the bone, on the shoulder, on the brow, on the knuckle:
Touch like a last name, touch like a wet match.
Touch like an empty shoe and an empty shoe, sweet
and incomprehensible. This ink. This name. This blood
and wonder. This box. This body in a box. This blood
in the body. This wind in the blood.

By Terrance Hayes

CHAPLINESQUE

We make our meek adjustments,
Contented with such random consolations
As the wind deposits
In slithered and too ample pockets.

For we can still love the world, who find
A famished kitten on the step, and know
Recesses for it from the fury of the street,
Or warm torn elbow coverts.

We will sidestep, and to the final smirk
Dally the doom of that inevitable thumb
That slowly chafes its puckered index toward us,
Facing the dull squint with what innocence
And what surprise!

And yet these fine collapses are not lies
More than the pirouettes of any pliant cane;
Our obsequies are, in a way, no enterprise.
We can evade you, and all else but the heart:
What blame to us if the heart live on.

The game enforces smirks; but we have seen
The moon in lonely alleys make
A grail of laughter of an empty ash can,
And through all sound of gaiety and quest
Have heard a kitten in the wilderness.

BY HART CRANE

WE ARE ONLY HUMAN

Nighttime amnesia.
The dream becoming
Cartoonish and mint-sequined.

A caboose climbing an emerald hill.
Daily we tend the garden.
Daily we wave

Our lashes like little flags
In a cordial wind. I? Who isn't
Ever I in a circular now.

The toothbrush is ready.
The mouth comes to meet it.
Life begins and goes on.

The fall is always waiting.
We're the always drifting above.

BY MARY JO BANG

THE BRAIN, WITHIN ITS GROOVE

The Brain, within its Groove
Runs evenly – and true –
But let a Splinter swerve –
'Twere easier for You –

To put a Current back –
When Floods have slit the Hills –
And scooped a Turnpike for Themselves –
And trodden out the Mills –

BY EMILY DICKINSON

ONE IS ONE

Heart, you bully, you punk, I'm wrecked, I'm shocked
stiff. You? you still try to rule the world—though
I've got you: identified, starving, locked
in a cage you will not leave alive, no
matter how you hate it, pound its walls,
& thrill its corridors with messages.

Brute. Spy. I trusted you. Now you reel & brawl
in your cell but I'm deaf to your rages,
your greed to go solo, your eloquent
threats of worse things you (knowing me) could do.
You scare me, bragging you're a double agent

since jailers are prisoners' prisoners too.
Think! Reform! Make us one. Join the rest of us,
and joy may come, and make its test of us.

BY MARIE PONSOT

FINITE AND INFINITE

The wind sounds only in opposing straits,
The sea, beside the shore; man's spirit rends
Its quiet only up against the ends
Of wants and oppositions, loves and hates,
Where, worked and worn by passionate debates,
And losing by the loss it apprehends,
The flesh rocks round, and every breath it sends
Is ravelled to a sigh. All tortured states
Suppose a straitened place. Jehovah Lord,
Make room for rest, around me! Out of sight
Now float me, of the vexing land abhorred,
Till in deep calms of space my soul may right
Her nature,—shoot large sail on lengthening cord,
And rush exultant on the Infinite.

BY ELIZABETH BARRETT BROWNING

Sonic Youth

Into the land of youth

Into the land of youth, westward, to the place of starting again, cities of gold, on the coast of promise—mysterious cure—a mirror's thrown down, and so without luck, without reflection we stop.

We have come to the beginning, the finish of the country, itinerary worn out, facing the surf—what sailors smell as land. We ask detailed questions. None of us can tell, so we tug on each other, "Come. Look."

In this lull, one at the tide line stoops to pick at foam and weeds; another builds a fire. The intended didn't arrive and there is no new plan. As the sun lowers, we face the mountains, consider what we have passed, and fall to dreaming, to scrounging.

By Killarney Clary

From GAMES WITH CHILDREN

red rover, red rover, why can't
you come over?
toward morning, toward evening,
why not let go —
and come over, come
over, why can't you
come over? red rover, red
rover, decider, permitter,
red rover, red rover,
why won't you let go?

BY SUSAN STEWART

THE SONG OF WANDERING AENGUS

I went out to the hazel wood,
Because a fire was in my head,
And cut and peeled a hazel wand,
And hooked a berry to a thread;
And when white moths were on the wing,
And moth-like stars were flickering out,
I dropped the berry in a stream
And caught a little silver trout.

When I had laid it on the floor
I went to blow the fire aflame,
But something rustled on the floor,
And some one called me by my name:
It had become a glimmering girl
With apple blossom in her hair
Who called me by my name and ran
And faded through the brightening air.

Though I am old with wandering
Through hollow lands and hilly lands,
I will find out where she has gone,
And kiss her lips and take her hands;
And walk among long dappled grass,
And pluck till time and times are done
The silver apples of the moon,
The golden apples of the sun.

By WILLIAM BUTLER YEATS

Anthem for Doomed Youth

What passing-bells for these who die as cattle?
Only the monstrous anger of the guns.
Only the stuttering rifles' rapid rattle
Can patter out their hasty orisons.
No mockeries now for them; no prayers nor bells;
Nor any voice of mourning save the choirs,
The shrill, demented choirs of wailing shells;
And bugles calling for them from sad shires.
What candles may be held to speed them all?
Not in the hands of boys, but in their eyes
Shall shine the holy glimmers of good-byes.
The pallor of girls' brows shall be their pall;
Their flowers the tenderness of patient minds,
And each slow dusk a drawing-down of blinds.

By Wilfred Owen

BY DAYLIGHT

In the tropical glass of a cool, foreign
mirror, I saw myself for the first time:
head forward on my unstraightened spine
from too much reading, cheeks scored

by impatience. I can never control
my eyes—gray, saddened at will,
with an uncurbed glare for looked-for double-dealing,
but still looking half a simpleton's after all.

And then, where the surface wavered,
I saw surprise—a sweating older woman, her coming
printed in faint lines around my mouth—and loved
the old bitch, whole, as if she were my next-door neighbor.

BY ELIZABETH MACKLIN

THE OLD MAN
AND THE MOTORCYCLE

The old man had inoperable cancer.
The old man's wife was dead
And the old man's kids didn't like him,

So the old man sold most everything
And bought a motorcycle
And the old man got back

To the backroads, to the roads he'd so
Enjoyed as a young man,
And the old man figured what the hell,

I'm sick I don't have long I might
As well die falling off this thing
Somewhere: this affordable, this moving,

This very roaring thing on these last roads.

By Liam Rector

MUZAK

When old, do not let me bark
at passersby—let me be

like the slow motion, down-
the-street dog, ignoring

the cardinals, the colors
he cannot see, even us

as we tiptoe by—
Friend, please save me

from being the neighbors'
fool hound who woofs loud

at every grey squirrel, stray
noise, or lab rushing past

to meet some lady—from being
that cur who cannot help but howl

all night like newlyweds
keeping the world awake. O terrible

angel of the elevator, the plane,
insufferable unquiet we pray to, afraid—

Please make me mild

BY KEVIN YOUNG

WEATHER

I had already begun
being a woman who lived
mostly alone, going *huh*
and piping, shuffling
through the rest
of her time. I contain
a running kid, a
green elf. I am
entirely alone. I desire
a certain sports car
a drippy night. Making
hairpin turns
in Rome your
face beams
up like a million
jiggling suns.

Do you get
it? Go.
what you
know is
true. I am so
long gone
down my
road.

BY EILEEN MYLES

FLOOD PLAIN

The red jacket waits in the closet to go by.
The lizard waits in the sunshine to go by.
Money, large denominations, waiting to go by.
Youth going by, the heart turns to solder
then no, a mimosa tree. Herd of elk, milk
on the shelf, the kingdom of the elf.
Piñatas going by. Wham, birthday boy
swats, scattering trinkets and sweets.
Flash going by the camera. 500 miles per hour
weekend, speed of light Dalmatian pup.
Great mental effort going by but not enough
to mend a string. In a red jacket, you go by,
the moment lost, firecracker gone off, just
gunpowder-smelling shreds. The day drags by
the moon then the moon returns as if looking
for its keys. On the table they wait
not going anywhere it seems to the naked
eye but actually flying by, flying apart,
made of atoms locked in repulsive force.
My buddy's son not six feet tall, took all
of what? twenty minutes. Stop! Hard not to want
to get a choke-hold on something anything,
a piece of bread, stay, it can't. Spring
throwing itself a parade as it goes by,
fire truck, veterans, jet plane, wedding
going by so long the end's a funeral.
Popsicle stick bumping down rain-glutted
gutter. Let it go, says the wise man,
lest you be too weighed down going
where you must go by.

By Dean Young

GROWN-UP

Was it for this I uttered prayers,
And sobbed and cursed and kicked the stairs,
That now, domestic as a plate,
I should retire at half-past eight?

BY EDNA ST. VINCENT MILLAY

THE LIGHTHOUSE KEEPER

My ear, a shell on the pillow;
      the down, the sea from which his mouth arrived.

Strange to live in a wet world, then wake in the desert.
      The cactus on whom milky needles grow.

Let me live offshore, where the water is low.
      Strange, and then so much less so.

I was seventeen. Do you want
      to know what I didn't know?

I do.

By Meghan O'Rourke

I Go Back to May 1937

I see them standing at the formal gates of their colleges,
I see my father strolling out
under the ochre sandstone arch, the
red tiles glinting like bent
plates of blood behind his head, I
see my mother with a few light books at her hip
standing at the pillar made of tiny bricks,
the wrought-iron gate still open behind her, its
sword-tips aglow in the May air,
they are about to graduate, they are about to get married,
they are kids, they are dumb, all they know is they are
innocent, they would never hurt anybody.
I want to go up to them and say Stop,
don't do it—she's the wrong woman,
he's the wrong man, you are going to do things
you cannot imagine you would ever do,
you are going to do bad things to children,
you are going to suffer in ways you have not heard of,
you are going to want to die. I want to go
up to them there in the late May sunlight and say it,
her hungry pretty face turning to me,
her pitiful beautiful untouched body,
his arrogant handsome face turning to me,
his pitiful beautiful untouched body,
but I don't do it. I want to live. I
take them up like the male and female
paper dolls and bang them together
at the hips, like chips of flint, as if to
strike sparks from them, I say
Do what you are going to do, and I will tell about it.

By Sharon Olds

THERE ARE TWO RIPENINGS

There are two Ripenings –
One – of Sight – whose Forces spheric wind
Until the Velvet Product
Drop, spicy, to the Ground –

A Homelier – maturing –
A Process in the Bur –
That Teeth of Frosts, alone disclose –
On far October Air –

By Emily Dickinson

WINTER FIELD

The winter field is not
the field of summer lost in snow: it is
another thing, a different thing.

"We shouted, we shook you," you tell me,
but there was no sound, no face, no fear, only
oblivion—why shouldn't it be so?

After they'd pierced a vein and fished me up,
after they'd reeled me back they packed me under
blanket on top of blanket, I trembled so.

The summer field, sun-fed, mutable,
has its many tasks; the winter field
becomes its adjective.
                        For those hours
I was some other thing, and my body,
which you have long loved well,
did not love you.

BY ELLEN BRYANT VOIGT

WHEN I CONSIDER
EVERY THING THAT GROWS

When I consider every thing that grows
Holds in perfection but a little moment.
That this huge stage presenteth nought but shows
Whereon the stars in secret influence comment.
When I perceive that men as plants increase,
Cheerèd and checked even by the self-same sky,
Vaunt in their youthful sap, at height decrease,
And wear their brave state out of memory;
Then the conceit of this inconstant stay,
Sets you most rich in youth before my sight,
Where wasteful Time debateth with decay
To change your day of youth to sullied night;
And all in war with Time for love of you,
As he takes from you, I engraft you new.

BY WILLIAM SHAKESPEARE

LAMENT FOR THE MAKERS

Not bird not badger not beaver not bee

Many creatures must
make, but only one must seek

within itself what to make

My father's ring was a *B* with a dart
through it, in diamonds against polished black stone.

I have it. What parents leave you
is their lives.

Until my mother died she struggled to make
a house that she did not loathe; paintings; poems; me.

Many creatures must

make, but only one must seek
within itself what to make

Not bird not badger not beaver not bee

*   *   *

Teach me, masters who by making were
remade, your art.

BY FRANK BIDART

From My Father's
Side of the Bed

When he had fallen deep asleep and was snoring
and I had moved out slowly from under his heavy arm,

I would sometimes nudge him a little,
not to wake him—

but so that he would sleep more lightly
and wake more easily should the soldiers,

maybe already assembling in the downstairs hall,
who were going to kill my father and rape my mother,

begin to mount the stairs.

By Marie Howe

THE MAN SPLITTING WOOD
IN THE DAYBREAK

The man splitting wood in the daybreak
looks strong, as though, if one weakened,
one could turn to him and he would help.
Gus Newland was strong. When he split wood
he struck hard, flashing the bright steel
through the air so hard the hard maple
leapt apart, as it's feared marriages will do
in countries reluctant to permit divorce,
and even willow, which, though stacked
to dry a full year, on being split
actually weeps—totem wood, therefore,
to the married-until-death—sunders
with many little lip-wetting gasp-noises.
But Gus is dead. We could turn to our fathers,
but they help us only by the unperplexed
looking-back of the numerals cut into headstones.
Or to our mothers, whose love, so devastated,
can't, even in spring, break through the hard earth.
Our spouses weaken at the same rate we do.
We have to hold our children up to lean on them.
Everyone who could help goes or hasn't arrived.
What about the man splitting wood in the daybreak,
who looked strong? That was years ago. That was me.

BY GALWAY KINNELL

THERE IS NEVER ENOUGH TIME

Above the clouds
is nothing
but a leprous
single star. (B. Brecht)

The more I look at it
the less I feel.
I try to recollect. I shake
a distant hand
& pay for laughter.
The odds are heavily
against me.
There is never enough time.
When I place a foot
in the hot water
someone declares me lost.
I smile into a mirror
& my face
glares back.
A father holds his babe
up to the light.
Where will it lead us?
Heaven is no place for fools.
I run my fingers
through your hair
& feel the universe
shut down.

BY JEROME ROTHENBERG

AFTER READING TU FU, I GO OUTSIDE TO THE DWARF ORCHARD

East of me, west of me, full summer.
How deeper than elsewhere the dusk is in your own yard.
Birds fly back and forth across the lawn

looking for home

As night drifts up like a little boat.

Day after day, I become of less use to myself.
Like this mockingbird,

I flit from one thing to the next.
What do I have to look forward to at fifty-four?
Tomorrow is dark.

Day-after-tomorrow is darker still.

The sky dogs are whimpering.
Fireflies are dragging the hush of evening

up from the damp grass.

Into the world's tumult, into the chaos of every day,
Go quietly, quietly.

By Charles Wright

SIX APOLOGIES, LORD

I Have Loved My Horrible Self, Lord.
I Rose, Lord, And I Rose, Lord, And I
Dropt. Your Requirements, Lord. 'Spite Your Requirements, Lord,
I Have Loved the Low Voltage Of The Moon, Lord,
Until There Was No Moon Intensity Left, Lord, No Moon
        Intensity Left
For You, Lord. I Have Loved The Frivolous, The Fleeting, The
        Frightful
Clouds, Lord. I Have Loved Clouds! Do Not Forgive Me, Do Not
Forgive Me LordandLover, HarborandMaster, GuardianandBread,
        Do Not.
Hold me, Lord, O, Hold Me

Accountable, Lord. I Am
Accountable. Lord.

Lord It Over Me,
Lord It Over Me, Lord. Feed Me

Hope, Lord. Feed Me
Hope, Lord, Or Break My Teeth.

Break My Teeth, Sir,

In This My Mouth.

BY OLENA KALYTIAK DAVIS

HIS EXCUSE FOR LOVING

Let it not your wonder move,
Less your laughter, that I love.
Though I now write fifty years,
I have had, and have, my peers.
Poets, though divine, are men;
Some have loved as old again.
And it is not always face,
Clothes, or fortune gives the grace,
Or the feature, or the youth;
But the language and the truth,
With the ardor and the passion,
Gives the lover weight and fashion.
If you then would hear the story,
First, prepare you to be sorry
That you never knew till now
Either whom to love or how;
But be glad as soon with me
When you hear that this is she
Of whose beauty it was sung,
She shall make the old man young,
Keep the middle age at stay,
And let nothing hide decay,
Till she be the reason why
All the world for love may die.

BY BEN JONSON

EROTIC ENERGY

Don't tell me we're not like plants,
sending out a shoot when we need to,
or spikes, poisonous oils, or flowers.

Come to me but only when I say,
that's how plants announce

the rules of propagation.
Even children know this. You can
see them imitating all the moves

with their bright plastic toys.
So that, years later, at the moment

the girl's body finally says yes
to the end of childhood,
a green pail with an orange shovel

will appear in her mind like a tropical
blossom she has never seen before.

BY CHASE TWICHELL

THE RED POPPY

The great thing
is not having
a mind. Feelings:
oh, I have those; they
govern me. I have
a lord in heaven
called the sun, and open
for him, showing him
the fire of my own heart, fire
like his presence.
What could such glory be
if not a heart? Oh my brothers and sisters,
were you like me once, long ago,
before you were human? Did you
permit yourselves
to open once, who would never
open again? Because in truth
I am speaking now
the way you do. I speak
because I am shattered.

BY LOUISE GLÜCK

LINES: "I AM"

I am—yet what I am, none cares or knows;
My friends forsake me like a memory lost:
I am the self-consumer of my woes—
They rise and vanish in oblivion's host
Like shadows in love-frenzied stifled throes—
And yet I am and live—like vapours tossed

Into the nothingness of scorn and noise,
Into the living sea of waking dreams
Where there is neither sense of life or joys
But the vast shipwreck of my life's esteems;
Even the dearest that I love the best
Are strange—nay, rather, stranger than the rest.

I long for scenes where man hath never trod,
A place where woman never smiled or wept,
There to abide with my Creator, God,
And sleep as I in childhood sweetly slept,
Untroubling and untroubled where I lie,
The grass below—above, the vaulted sky.

BY JOHN CLARE

City, My City

From THE INVENTION
OF STREETLIGHTS

noctes illustratas
(the night has houses)
                          and the shadow of the fabulous
                  broken into handfuls—these
can be placed at regular intervals,
                                    candles
walking down streets at times eclipsed by trees.

BY COLE SWENSEN

From MANNAHATTA

Now I see what there is in a name, a word, liquid, sane, unruly,
    musical, self-sufficient,
I see that the word of my city is that word from of old,
Because I see that word nested in nests of water-bays, superb,
Rich, hemm'd thick all around with sailships and steamships, an
    island sixteen miles long, solid-founded,
Numberless crowded streets, high growths of iron, slender, strong,
    light, splendidly uprising toward clear skies,
Tides swift and ample, well-loved by me, toward sundown,
The flowing sea-currents, the little islands, larger adjoining islands,
    the heights, the villas,
The countless masts, the white shore-steamers, the lighters, the
    ferry-boats, the black sea-steamers well-model'd,
The down-town streets, the jobbers' houses of business, the houses of
    business of the ship-merchants and money-brokers, the river-
    streets,
Immigrants arriving, fifteen or twenty thousand in a week,
The carts hauling goods, the manly race of drivers of horses, the
    brown-faced sailors,
The summer air, the bright sun shining, and the sailing clouds aloft,
The winter snows, the sleigh-bells, the broken ice in the river, passing
    along up or down with the flood-tide or ebb-tide,
The mechanics of the city, the masters, well-form'd, beautiful-faced,
    looking you straight in the eyes,
Trottoirs throng'd, vehicles, Broadway, the women, the shops and
    shows,
A million people—manners free and superb—open voices—hospitality
    —the most courageous and friendly young men,
City of hurried and sparkling waters! city of spires and masts!
City nested in bays! my city!

BY WALT WHITMAN

The Empire State Building
Is on 63rd Street
Ramon wanted to bet Manolo
Manolo said impossible
The Empire State Building
Is on 72nd Street
They made a ten dollar bet
And borrowed Cheo's car
And headed towards Brooklin
When they came back
Late that night
All that Manolo wanted to know
Was
If Gloria cooked

BY VICTOR HERNÁNDEZ CRUZ

From THE CITY
IN WHICH I LOVE YOU

Morning comes to this city vacant of you.
Pages and windows flare, and you are not there.
Someone sweeps his portion of sidewalk,
wakens the drunk, slumped like laundry,
and you are gone.

You are not in the wind
which someone notes in the margins of a book.
You are gone out of the small fires in abandoned lots
where human figures huddle,
each aspiring to its own ghost.

Between brick walls, in a space no wider than my face,
a leafless sapling stands in mud.
In its branches, a nest of raw mouths
gaping and cheeping, scrawny fires that must eat.
My hunger for you is no less than theirs.

BY LI-YOUNG LEE

To One Who Has Been
Long in City Pent

To one who has been long in city pent,
      'Tis very sweet to look into the fair
      And open face of heaven,—to breathe a prayer
Full in the smile of the blue firmament.
Who is more happy, when, with heart's content,
      Fatigued he sinks into some pleasant lair
      Of wavy grass, and reads a debonair
And gentle tale of love and languishment?
Returning home at evening, with an ear
      Catching the notes of Philomel,—an eye
Watching the sailing cloudlet's bright career,
      He mourns that day so soon has glided by:
E'en like the passage of an angel's tear
      That falls through the clear ether silently.

By John Keats

THE TROPICS IN NEW YORK

Bananas ripe and green, and ginger-root,
    Cocoa in pods and alligator pears,
And tangerines and mangoes and grape fruit,
    Fit for the highest prize at parish fairs,

Set in the window, bringing memories
    Of fruit-trees laden by low-singing rills,
And dewy dawns, and mystical blue skies
    In benediction over nun-like hills.

My eyes grew dim, and I could no more gaze;
    A wave of longing through my body swept,
And, hungry for the old, familiar ways,
    I turned aside and bowed my head and wept.

By Claude McKay

HENRY HATES THE WORLD

Henry hates the world. What the world to Henry
did will not bear thought.
Feeling no pain,
Henry stabbed his arm and wrote a letter
explaining how bad it had been
in this world.

Old yellow, in a gown
might have made a difference, 'these lower beauties',
and chartreuse could have mattered

"Kyoto, Toledo,
Benares—the holy cities—
and Cambridge shimmering do not make up
for, well, the horror of unlove,
nor south from Paris driving in the Spring
to Siena and on . . ."

Pulling together Henry, somber Henry
woofed at things.
Spry disappointments of men
and vicing adorable children
miserable women, Henry mastered, Henry
tasting all the secret bits of life.

By John Berryman

THE TAXI

When I go away from you
The world beats dead
Like a slackened drum.
I call out for you against the jutted stars
And shout into the ridges of the wind.
Streets coming fast,
One after the other,
Wedge you away from me,
And the lamps of the city prick my eyes
So that I can no longer see your face.
Why should I leave you,
To wound myself upon the sharp edges of the night?

By Amy Lowell

100 RIVERSIDE: WAKING UP AT MARI'S

The city through her back-bedroom window: a shift-
ing of trash cans (snow-crunch of galvanized steel), gear
sounds drowned in metal hulls, horns now: one by one to lift,
fine-tune, and weigh my home town: *here, here!*

I let go, as passivest listeners listen, to sift
the city, naming sounds, for named sounds near
or distant make a depth where my too deft
attention—deep and troubled, city too endeared—

can lose itself. Always to arrive, and hear
on such first wakings everything that lives
within me sigh, as if to say *all's well, all's here,*

as if the old rifts in this reft
being were annealed. —AS IF is what it is. It's theft
of all that is. And nothing else is dear.

By Anne Winters

O WOOLLY CITY

O Woolly City, each thing dings dully as an acorn
And nothing that's glittery-clad, no sting, is found: swan-necked
Flasks (for don't we all crave beauty and contamination)
Aren't, and faetted gold's drammed with the gorgeous salts underground
Where love's brooklike dagger shivers. Drat love's daggery thirst.
And drat this woolliness: I promise you that there'll be facts
But many other things are, City, necessary first
And a person's in my pent house. A person or a spook
Who flits from opaque to Opaque. Away! And *segue*
In ultima; say our knees hurt and our elbows and backs;
Say it's growth phrasing its formal demands; say our bodies
As they each stand now, are the volumes of how, in the past,
They gave one graceful reply after the next…. Lover's love,
Till the last word unproofed is, say, pretext: a romance of
Manner. Say, Man or Ghost, more exactly: how difficult it is
To learn to speak our language fluently and correctly!

BY PRISCILLA SNEFF

BROKEN SONNET

The world weeps. There are no tears
To be found. It is deemed a miracle.
The president appears on screens
In villages and towns, in cities in jungles
And jungles still affectionately called cities.
He appears on screens and reads a story.
Whose story is he reading and why?
What lessons are to be learned from this story
About a time that has not arrived, will not arrive, is here?
Time of fire and images of fire climbing toward the sun
Time of precious and semi-precious liquids
Time of a man and a woman doused in ink
Rolling across streams and down valleys
Trying to leave some string of words behind.

BY JOHN YAU

IN ANTIGUA

*"In Antigua I am famous. I am bathed in jasmine
and pressed with warm stones."*
–Carnival Cruise ad in the *New Yorker*

In Albuquerque, on the other hand, I am infamous; children
throw stones and the elderly whisper behind their hands.
In Juneau, I am glacial, a cool blue where anyone can bathe
for a price. In Rio I am neither exalted nor defamed; I walk
the streets and nothing makes sense, voices garbled, something
about electricity, something about peonies and cheap wool.

In Prague I am as fabulous as Napoleon and everyone
knows it. They give me a horse and I tell them this horse
will be buried with me, I tell them I will call the horse either
Andromeda or Murphy and all applaud wildly. In Montreal
I am paler than I am in Toronto. In Istanbul I trip over cracks
in the sidewalk and no one rushes to take my elbow, to say
Miss or brew strong tea for a poultice. In Sydney they talk
about my arrival for days. I sit outside the opera house
waiting for miracles, and when none occur in a fortnight

it's Ecuador, where the old gods include the small scythes
of my fingernails in their rituals and I learn that anything
can ferment, given opportunity, given terra cotta. In Paris
I'm up all night. Off the Gold Coast, I marry a reverend
who swears that pelicans are god's birds and numbers them
fervently, meanwhile whistling. Near Bucharest I go all
invisible, also clammy, also way more earnest than I ever was
in Memphis. For three Sundays I wander skinny side streets
saying *amphora, amphora.*

By KERRI WEBSTER

THE HUNGARIAN PASTRY SHOP & CAFÉ

is the only place I know in the city
where you can still see people with pen
and paper. Legal pads, spiral bound,
plain or college-ruled loose leaf, well-thumbed sheaves
of paper at every crumb-strewn table: précis,
postulations, undergraduate observations, sound
doctoral theory, a shady spot of fiction—
each hand the only one in the world
to produce such symbols, personal as finger-
prints, errant *y*'s and flighty *t*'s,
g's trailing their tails like apprehensive
dogs. It's a deep, low-ceilinged room, illuminated
dimly by porcelain snowdrops on the walls,
a foreign spring, ripe with words' secret burning.

BY ANNE PIERSON WIESE

THE GREAT FIGURE

Among the rain
and lights
I saw the figure 5
in gold
on a red
firetruck
moving
tense
unheeded
to gong clangs
siren howls
and wheels rumbling
through the dark city.

BY WILLIAM CARLOS WILLIAMS

THE WHITE CITY

I will not toy with it nor bend an inch.
Deep in the secret chambers of my heart
I muse my life-long hate, and without flinch
I bear it nobly as I live my part.
My being would be a skeleton, a shell,
If this dark Passion that fills my every mood,
And makes my heaven in the white world's hell,
Did not forever feed me vital blood.
I see the mighty city through a mist—
The strident trains that speed the goaded mass,
The poles and spires and towers vapor-kissed,
The fortressed port through which the great ships pass,
The tides, the wharves, the dens I contemplate,
Are sweet like wanton loves because I hate.

By Claude McKay

SIDE 32

I am glad that I am not one of those
Big Con Edison pipes that sits by the
River crying smoke
I am glad that I am not the doorknob
Of a police car patrolling the Lower
East Side
How cool I am not a subway token
That has been lost and is sitting
Quietly and lonely by the edge of
A building on 47th Street
I am nothing and no one
I am the possibility of everything
I am a man in this crazy city
I am a door and a glass of water
I am a guitar string cutting through the
Smog
Vibrating and bringing morning
My head is a butterfly
Over the traffic jams.

BY VICTOR HERNÁNDEZ CRUZ

From CROSSING BROOKLYN FERRY

Flood-tide below me! I see you face to face!
Clouds of the west—sun there half an hour high—I see you also face to face.

Crowds of men and women attired in the usual costumes, how curious you
    are to me!
On the ferry-boats the hundreds and hundreds that cross, returning home,
    are more curious to me than you suppose,
And you that shall cross from shore to shore years hence are more to me, and
    more in my meditations, than you might suppose.

BY WALT WHITMAN

CATWALK

Every sidewalk's a treadmill
Meandering along a ripple & strut
Of flesh beneath the metaphysics
Of cloth or lack of. Somewhere

A hurricane off the coast of Africa
Heads to the Caribbean, to the Gulf...
Can jeans & short dresses take our minds
Off magma beneath the fox-trot & tango,

Runaway asteroids jiggling bones
Like worry beads on photo shoots?
But the gods are never caught
Crawling from top-notch machines,

& memory's broken skull lingers
On every corner where dogs are
Bred into distinction & beauty is
Praised down to the worm in the ark.

By Yusef Komunyakaa

FEAR

I am afraid of nature
because of nature   I am mortal

my children and my grandchildren
are also mortal

I lived in the city for forty years
in this way I escaped fear

BY GRACE PALEY

COYOTES IN GREENWICH!

Here hedges are upholstered, each cobblestone
has an appointment, greening boughs aspire
in vain to Tudor style while even ramblers
know their place. And yet, we saw hibiscus
in high alarm, cat-slunk shivering it.

Coyotes invade. They claim to be the truth.
Black bears nose the bougainvillea, moving
eastward, indiscriminate, original.
Our sinks back up, our toilets will not drain,
our nature disobediently tends toward nature.

But we will have no blame, for we attend
our garbage as we always have, bury
and send away what could not prosper Here.
In children's books we keep foxes and mice;
where are the Apaches to back us up?

Logically we sleep, though not in comfort
these days. Our wives keep turning in our beds
like roasting meat, the stones call out to us,
campfires fringe the Merritt. In our kitchens
pasta forks bare fangs, pans hang like scalps.

BY JULIE SHEEHAN

DSS Dream

I dreamed
the Department of Social Services
came to the door and said:
"We understand
you have a baby,
a goat, and a pig living here
in a two-room apartment.
This is illegal.
We have to take the baby away,
unless you eat the goat."

"The pig's OK?" I asked.
"The pig's OK," they said.

By Martín Espada

HARM

With his shopping cart, his bags of booty and his wine, I'd
always found him inoffensive.
Every neighborhood has one or two these days; ours never
rants at you at least or begs.

He just forages the trash all day, drinks and sings and
shadowboxes, then at nightfall
finds a doorway to make camp, set out his battered little radio
and slab of rotting foam.

The other day, though, as I was going by, he stepped abruptly
out between parked cars,
undid his pants, and, not even bothering to squat, sputtered
out a noxious, almost liquid stream.

There was that, and that his bony shanks and buttocks were
already stained beyond redemption,
that his scarlet testicles were blown up bigger than a bull's
with some sorrowful disease,

and that a slender adolescent girl from down the block
happened by right then, and looked,
and looked away, and looked at me, and looked away again,
and made me want to say to her,

because I imagined what she must have felt, It's not like this,
really, it's not this,
but she was gone, so I could think, But isn't it like this, isn't
this just what it is?

By C. K. Williams

SHARKS' TEETH

Everything contains some
silence. Noise gets
its zest from the
small shark's-tooth
shaped fragments
of rest angled
in it. An hour
of city holds maybe
a minute of these
remnants of a time
when silence reigned,
compact and dangerous
as a shark. Sometimes
a bit of a tail
or fin can still
be sensed in parks.

By Kay Ryan

MEAT

How much meat moves
Into the city each night
The decks of its bridges tremble
In the liquefaction of sodium light
And the moon a chemical orange

Semitrailers strain their axles
Shivering as they take the long curve
Over warehouses and lofts
The wilderness of streets below
The mesh of it
With Joe on the front stoop smoking
And Louise on the phone with her mother

Out of the haze of industrial meadows
They arrive, numberless
Hauling tons of dead lamb
Bone and flesh and offal
Miles to the ports and channels
Of the city's shimmering membrane
A giant breathing cell
Exhaling its waste
From the stacks by the river
And feeding through the night

By August Kleinzahler

TRANSCONTINENT

Where the cities end, the
dumps grow the oil-can shacks,
from Portland, Maine,

to Seattle. Broken
cars rust in Troy, New York,
and Cleveland Heights.

On the train, the people
eat candy bars, and watch,
or fall asleep.

When they look outside and
see cars and shacks, they know
they're nearly there.

BY DONALD HALL

Spring & After

TALLY-O

What ho! the wind is up and eloquent.
Through all the Winter's halls he crieth Spring.
Now will I get me up unto mine own forests
And behold their bourgeoning.

BY EZRA POUND

SPRING

To what purpose, April, do you return again?
Beauty is not enough.
You can no longer quiet me with the redness
Of little leaves opening stickily.
I know what I know.
The sun is hot on my neck as I observe
The spikes of the crocus.
The smell of the earth is good.
It is apparent that there is no death.
But what does that signify?
Not only under ground are the brains of men
Eaten by maggots.
Life in itself
Is nothing,
An empty cup, a flight of uncarpeted stairs.
It is not enough that yearly, down this hill,
April
Comes like an idiot, babbling and strewing flowers.

By Edna St. Vincent Millay

THE TREES

The trees are coming into leaf
Like something almost being said;
The recent buds relax and spread,
Their greenness is a kind of grief.

Is it that they are born again
And we grow old? No, they die too.
Their yearly trick of looking new
Is written down in rings of grain.

Yet still the unresting castles thresh
In fullgrown thickness every May.
Last year is dead, they seem to say,
Begin afresh, afresh, afresh.

BY PHILIP LARKIN

A LITTLE MADNESS IN THE SPRING

A little Madness in the Spring
Is wholesome even for the King,
But God be with the Clown –
Who ponders this tremendous scene –
This whole Experiment of Green –
As if it were his own!

BY EMILY DICKINSON

FROM YOU HAVE I BEEN
ABSENT IN THE SPRING

From you have I been absent in the spring,
When proud-pied April, dressed in all his trim,
Hath put a spirit of youth in everything,
That heavy Saturn laughed and leaped with him,
Yet nor the lays of birds, nor the sweet smell
Of different flowers in odor and in hue,
Could make me any summer's story tell,
Or from their proud lap pluck them where they grew.
Nor did I wonder at the lily's white,
Nor praise the deep vermilion in the rose;
They were but sweet, but figures of delight,
Drawn after you, you pattern of all those.
    Yet seemed it winter still, and, you away,
    As with your shadow I with these did play.

BY WILLIAM SHAKESPEARE

I SHALL NOT CARE

When I am dead and over me bright April
    Shakes out her rain-drenched hair,
Tho' you should lean above me broken-hearted,
    I shall not care.

I shall have peace, as leafy trees are peaceful
    When rain bends down the bough,
And I shall be more silent and cold-hearted
    Than you are now.

BY SARA TEASDALE

LIKE RAIN IT SOUNDED
TILL IT CURVED

Like Rain it sounded till it curved
And then we knew 'twas Wind –
It walked as wet as any Wave
But swept as dry as Sand –
When it had pushed itself away
To some remotest Plain
A coming as of Hosts was heard
That was indeed the Rain –
It filled the Wells, it pleased the Pools
It warbled in the Road –
It pulled the spigot from the Hills
And let the Floods abroad –
It loosened acres, lifted seas
The sites of Centres stirred
Then like Elijah rode away
Opon a Wheel of Cloud –

BY EMILY DICKINSON

THE WINDHOVER

Caught this morning morning's minion, king-
    dom of daylight's dauphin, dapple-dawn-drawn Falcon, in his riding
    Of the rolling level underneath him steady air, and striding
High there, how he rung upon the rein of a wimpling wing
In his ecstasy! then off, off forth on swing,
    As a skate's heel sweeps smooth on a bow-bend: the hurl and gliding
    Rebuffed the big wind. My heart in hiding
Stirred for a bird,—the achieve of; the mastery of the thing!

Brute beauty and valour and act, oh, air, pride, plume, here
    Buckle! AND the fire that breaks from thee then, a billion
Times told lovelier, more dangerous, O my chevalier!

    No wonder of it: shéer plód makes plough down sillion
Shine, and blue-bleak embers, ah my dear,
    Fall, gall themselves, and gash gold-vermillion.

BY GERARD MANLEY HOPKINS

WATER RAINING

Water astonishing and difficult altogether makes a meadow and a stroke.

BY GERTRUDE STEIN

WHEN ECSTASY IS INCONVENIENT

Feign a great calm;
all gay transport soon ends.
Chant: who knows—
flight's end or flight's beginning
for the resting gull?

Heart, be still.
Say there is money but it rusted;
say the time of moon is not right for escape.
It's the color in the lower sky
too broadly suffused,
or the wind in my tie.

Know amazedly how
often one takes his madness
into his own hands
and keeps it.

BY LORINE NIEDECKER

AT THE END OF SUMMER
for Louis Zukofsky

Go on
Mr. Tree Fugue
I'm listening.

BY ELAINE EQUI

THE SHEAVES

Where long the shadows of the wind had rolled,
Green wheat was yielding to the change assigned;
And as by some vast magic undivined
The world was turning slowly into gold.
Like nothing that was ever bought or sold
It waited there, the body and the mind;
And with a mighty meaning of a kind
That tells the more the more it is not told.

So in a land where all days are not fair,
Fair days went on till on another day
A thousand golden sheaves were lying there,
Shining and still, but not for long to stay—
As if a thousand girls with golden hair
Might rise from where they slept and go away.

BY EDWIN ARLINGTON ROBINSON

So I Will Till the Ground

So I will furrow the garden beds
with hook and spade
lay the edge of my hand
into the moistest soil

So I will plant artichoke and wild mint
because they are the splendors of any table
I will rejoice in carrot and radish
because they are the earth's own kind

So I will mulch the seedling tomato
that was my grandfather's preference
scatter caraway and clove
to retrieve the spices of his pleasure

So I will shepherd the turnips for my great aunt
who loved their soundness
I will induce the oleander to proliferate
among the four corners of my tending

So I will dig, perforate, hoe, scarify,
that out of these many wounds
there might come flower and fruit
to carry forth, to replenish.

By Gregory Djanikian

THE SEASONS

Ice-jammed hard-clasped branches in the blocks a whole river of them
    yet at the same time, the time sensed
beneath the time walked, the time breathing in and out, the water
       almost
     eddying, still pushing there beneath
the milk-white surface, deep down and over the bed of rocks; you
       could call
    them frozen, though they never live
another state than less and less until they're gone, the water going on
      and on
     until it all accrues again. The seasons
always seemed to be a form of freedom, something good for making
      meaning,
    the kind of notion a founding father could
pull out now and then whenever
    the now and then would flag. Time
healing time, you know the saw.
    Lightning strikes and struck.
The shepherd fell down dead.
And then it all wound up again: a redbreast made a ruckus, the quick
      eternal sprung.

You wanted summer or you wanted death.
So death came again, and that was autumn.

BY SUSAN STEWART

September, Inverness

Tomales Bay is flat blue in the Indian summer heat.
This is the time when hikers on Inverness Ridge
Stand on tiptoe to pick ripe huckleberries
That the deer can't reach. This is the season of lulls—
Egrets hunting in the tidal shallows, a ribbon
Of sandpipers fluttering over mudflats, white,
Then not. A drift of mist wisping off the bay.
This is the moment when bliss is what you glimpse
From the corner of your eye, as you drive past
Running errands, and the wind comes up,
And the surface of the water glitters hard against it.

By Robert Hass

WE HAVE THE RIGHT
TO LOVE AUTUMN

And we, too, have the right to love the last days of autumn and ask the grove:
Is there room now for a new autumn, so we may lie down like coals?
Like gold, autumn brings its leaves to half-staff.
If only we never said goodbye to the fundamentals
and questioned our fathers when they fled at knife-point.

   May poetry and God's name have mercy on us!
We have the right to warm the nights of beautiful women, and talk about
what might shorten the night of two strangers waiting for North on the compass.
It's autumn. We have the right to smell autumn's fragrances

   and ask the night for a dream.
Does the dream, like the dreamers themselves, sicken? *Autumn. Autumn.*
Can a people be born on a guillotine?
We have the right to die any way we wish.
May the earth hide itself away in a blade of wheat!

BY MAHMOUD DARWISH
TRANSLATED FROM THE ARABIC BY MUNIR AKASH AND CAROLYN FORCHÉ

Spellbound

The night is darkening round me,
The wild winds coldly blow;
But a tyrant spell has bound me
And I cannot, cannot go.

The giant trees are bending
Their bare boughs weighed with snow.
And the storm is fast descending,
And yet I cannot go.

Clouds beyond clouds above me,
Wastes beyond wastes below;
But nothing dear can move me;
I will not, cannot go.

By Emily Brontë

HOW LONELY IT IS

How lonely it is:
The snowstorm has made the world
    The size of my yard.

BY RICHARD WRIGHT

Bloom

There are canisters of kerosene
burning a path across the ice
taken from the kitchen store
and put there in two long rows—

midnight-blue, penguin-starred
briefly interrupted. We live
underground because it's warmer.
We've heard news of a Great Schism

and that the Old Calendarists
have not forgotten a certain slight
and of a church infested by bees
how honey runs from the walls.

By Lisa Olstein

WINTRY MIX

The 6 A.M. January
encaustic clouds
are built
in a waxy gray putty
whizzing by with spots
of luminous silvery
crack-o'-the-world light
coming through, an eerie
end-o'-the-world feeling
yet reassuring
like an old movie.
Do I really have to go out there?
Now a hint of muted
salmon tones breaking
a warmish band
of welcoming pinkish light.
Is it like this every morning?
My head still in the dark.
Worry, eck! But the brightening
russet tipped cloud ballet
reminds me of something
in Pliny, yea, Pliny.
Can't imagine opening
the door today in a toga.
Work and more,
yes, work
sends us into the draft.

BY PETER GIZZI

DECEMBER

I will sleep
in my little cup

BY RON PADGETT

THE DARKLING THRUSH

I leant upon a coppice gate
 When Frost was spectre-gray,
And Winter's dregs made desolate
 The weakening eye of day.
The tangled bine-stems scored the sky
 Like strings of broken lyres,
And all mankind that haunted nigh
 Had sought their household fires.

The land's sharp features seemed to be
 The Century's corpse outleant,
His crypt the cloudy canopy,
 The wind his death-lament.
The ancient pulse of germ and birth
 Was shrunken hard and dry,
And every spirit upon earth
 Seemed fervourless as I.

At once a voice arose among
 The bleak twigs overhead
In a full-hearted evensong
 Of joy illimited;
An aged thrush, frail, gaunt, and small,
 In blast-beruffled plume,
Had chosen thus to fling his soul
 Upon the growing gloom.

So little cause for carolings
 Of such ecstatic sound
Was written on terrestrial things
 Afar or nigh around,
That I could think there trembled through
 His happy good-night air
Some blessed Hope, whereof he knew
 And I was unaware.

BY THOMAS HARDY

THE DAY OF COLD FOOD

Clear and bright is the splendor
Of Spring on the Day of Cold Food.
The dying smoke rises from
The jade animal like a
Silk thread floating in water.
I dream on a pile of cushions,
Amongst scattered and broken hair ornaments.
The swallows have not come back
From the Southern Sea, but already
Men begin again, fighting for straws.
Petals fly from the peach trees
Along the river. Willow catkins
Fill the air with floss. And then—
In the orange twilight—fall
Widely spaced drops of rain.

By Li Ch'ing Chao
translated from the Chinese by Kenneth Rexroth

AUBADE

Summer and winter over the lakes and earth.
In silence the women slide over ice, lines
drop off their heels and the cutting sound
of stops. *Not*
this way they think under stars, although
inside there is confusion, shame,
materials for beginning, a body
out of which comes everything that eventually
cannot endure. Summers they sit
with children reading *black sea*
carries the ship until rain dents the mud.
What calls us is not the riot of love
but the hollowness that stays here as we
lean into the words, white blanket warming
at the work of such still bodies.

BY JOANNA KLINK

THE HUMAN SEASONS

Four seasons fill the measure of the year;
    There are four seasons in the mind of man:
He has his lusty Spring, when fancy clear
    Takes in all beauty with an easy span:
He has his Summer, when luxuriously
    Spring's honeyed cud of youthful thought he loves
To ruminate, and by such dreaming high
    Is nearest unto Heaven: quiet coves
His soul has in its Autumn, when his wings
    He furleth close; contented so to look
On mists in idleness—to let fair things
    Pass by unheeded as a threshold brook.
He has his Winter too of pale misfeature,
Or else he would forego his mortal nature.

BY JOHN KEATS

ACKNOWLEDGMENTS

The editor is grateful to Tree Swenson and the staff of the Academy of American Poets for launching the first national Poem in Your Pocket celebration during National Poetry Month in 2007. Many thanks to the New York City Department of Cultural Affairs for hosting and encouraging New Yorkers to put a poem in their pocket on Poem in Your Pocket Day every April since 2003.

Grateful acknowledgment is made to the publications in which the poems appear. Although every effort has been made to trace and contact copyright holders, in a few instances this has not been possible. If notified, the publishers will be pleased to rectify any omission in future editions.

LOVE & ROCKETS

"Catch" from *The Collected Poems of Langston Hughes* by Langston Hughes. Copyright © 1994 by the Estate of Langston Hughes. Used by permission of Alfred A Knopf, a division of Random House, Inc.

"Toe the Line with Me" from *Sad Little Breathing Machine* by Matthea Harvey, published by Graywolf Press. Copyright © 2004 by Graywolf Press. All rights reserved. Used with permission.

"Kore" from *The Collected Poems of Robert Creeley, 1975-2005* by Robert Creeley. Published by University of California Press. Copyright © 2008 by University of California Press. All rights reserved. Used with permission.

Poem XVII of "Twenty-One Love Poems." Copyright © 2002 by Adrienne Rich. Copyright © 1978 by W.W. Norton & Company, Inc., from *The Fact of a Doorframe: Selected Poems 1950-2001* by Adrienne Rich. Used by Permission of the author and W.W. Norton & Company, Inc.

"A Map of Love" from *Summer Anniversaries* by Donald Justice, published by Alfred A. Knopf, a division of Random House, Inc. Copyright © 1959 by Alfred A. Knopf, a division of Random House, Inc. All rights reserved. Used with permission of Alfred A. Knopf, a division of Random House, Inc.

"The More Loving One" from *Collected Poems* by W.H. Auden, published by Vintage Books, a division of Random House, Inc. Copyright © 1940 by Curtis Brown, Ltd. All rights reserved. Used with permission.

"Summer in a Small Town" from *Too Bright to See & Alma* by Linda Gregg, published by Graywolf Press. Copyright © 2001 by Graywolf Press. All rights reserved. Used with permission.

"Comment" from *The Portable Dorothy Parker* by Dorothy Parker, published by Viking Penguin, a division of Penguin Group (USA) Inc. Copyright © 1926 renewed 1954 by Dorothy Parker. All rights reserved. Used with permission of Viking Penguin.

"Juventius, honey-pot, I snatched from you while you were playing" from *The Poems of Catullus: A Bilingual Edition* by Gaius Valerius Catullus, edited and translated by Peter Green, published by University of California Press. Copyright © 2006 by Peter Green. Used with permission.

"Runaways Café II" from *Love, Death, and the Changing of the Seasons* by Marilyn Hacker, published by W.W. Norton & Company. Copyright © 1995 by W.W. Norton & Company. All rights reserved. Used by permission of the author.

"The Guests" from *The Lost Pilot by James Tate*, published by The Ecco Press. Copyright © 1967 by The Ecco Press. All rights reserved. Used with permission.

"The Dream" from *The Blue Estuaries: Poems 1923-1968* by Louise Bogan, published by Farrar, Straus, and Giroux. Copyright © 1995 by Farrar, Straus, and Giroux. All rights reserved. Used with permission.

"The Fist" from *Collected Poems, 1948-1984* by Derek Walcott, published by Farrar, Straus, and Giroux. Copyright © 1987 by Farrar, Straus, and Giroux. All rights reserved. Used with permission.

From "Time" and "A Good Time" from *Yehuda Amichai: A Life in Poetry 1948-1994* by Yehuda Amichai, translated by Benjamin and Barbara Harshav, published by Harper Perennial. Copyright © 1995 by HarperCollins Publishers. All rights reserved. Used with permission.

"Paradise Motel" from *A Wedding in Hell* by Charles Simic, published by Harcourt. Copyright © 1994 by Charles Simic. All rights reserved. Used by permission of the author.

From "The Reef" in *The Reef* by Elizabeth Arnold, published by University of Chicago Press. Copyright © 1999 by Elizabeth Arnold. All rights reserved. Used with permission.

"since feeling is first" from *Complete Poems 1904-1962* by E.E. Cummings, edited by George J. Firmage. Copyright 1923, 1925, 1951, 1951, © 1991 by the Trustees for the E. E. Cummings Trust. Copyright © 1976 by George James Firmage.

From "To Marina" from *The Collected Poems of Kenneth Koch* by Kenneth Koch , published by Alfred A. Knopf, a division of Random House, Inc. Copyright © 2007 by the Estate of Kenneth Koch. All rights reserved. Used with permission of Alfred A. Knopf, a division of Random House, Inc.

"You're" from *Collected Poems* by Sylvia Plath, published by Harper Perennial. Copyright © 1960, 1965, 1971, 1981 by the Estate of Sylvia Plath. Editorial matter copyright © 1981 by Ted Hughes. All rights reserved. Used with permission.

"Meditation on Falling" from *Into Perfect Spheres Such Holes Are Pierced* by Catherine Barnett, published by Alice James Books. Copyright © 2004 by Alice James Books. Used by permission of the author and Alice James Books.

DWELLINGS

"Father's Bedroom" from *Collected Poems* by Robert Lowell, published by Farrar, Straus, and Giroux. Copyright © 2003 by Farrar, Straus, and Giroux. All rights reserved. Used with permission.

From "The God of Windowscreens and Honeysuckle" in *Shadows of Houses* by H.L.Hix, published by Etruscan Press. Copyright © 2005 by Etruscan Press. All rights reserved. Used by permission of the author.

"Bell Pepper" from *The World at Large* by James McMichael, published by University of Chicago Press. Copyright © 2006 by University of Chicago Press. All rights reserved. Used by permission of the author.

"The Cabbage" from *In the Next Galaxy* by Ruth Stone, published by Copper Canyon Press. Copyright © 2004 by Copper Canyon Press. All rights reserved. Used with permission.

"Loft" from *Collected Poems 1951-1971* by A.R. Ammons, published by W.W. Norton & Company. Copyright © 2001 by W.W. Norton & Company. All rights reserved. Used with permission.

"Tent" from *Hum* by Ann Lauterbach, published by Penguin Group (USA), Inc. Copyright © 2005 by Penguin Group (USA), Inc. All rights reserved. Used by permission of Penguin Group (USA), Inc.

From "The Cell" in *The Cell by Lyn Hejinian*, published by Sun & Moon Press. Copyright © 1992 by Lyn Hejinian. All rights reserved. Used with permission.

"Leave-Taking" from *Invisible Tender* by Jennifer Clarvoe, published by Fordham University Press. Copyright © 2000 by Fordham University Press. All rights reserved. Used by permission of the author.

"Home is So Sad" from *Collected Poems* by Philip Larkin, published by Farrar, Straus, and Giroux. Copyright © 2004 by Farrar, Straus, and Giroux. All rights reserved. Used with permission.

"Sleeping on the Ceiling" from *The Complete Poems: 1927-1979* by Elizabeth Bishop, published by Farrar, Straus, and Giroux. Copyright © 1984 by Farrar, Straus, and Giroux. All rights reserved. Used with permission.

"The Window" from *The Collected Poems of Robert Creeley, 1975-2005* by Robert Creeley, published by University of California Press. Copyright © 2008 by University of California Press. All rights reserved. Used with permission.

"Child on Top of a Greenhouse" from *Collected Poems* by Theodore Roethke, published by Anchor Books, a division of Random House, Inc. Copyright © 1974 by Anchor Books, a division of Random House, Inc. All rights reserved. Used with permission.

"Entrance" from *Divide These* by Saskia Hamilton, published by Graywolf Press. Copyright © 2005 by Graywolf Press. All rights reserved. Used with permission of Graywolf Press.

"On Being a Householder" from *Poems Seven: New and Complete Poetry* by Alan Dugan, published by Seven Stories Press.Copyright © 2003 by the Estate of Alan Dugan. All rights reserved. Used with permission.

"Desert Places" from *The Poetry of Robert Frost*, edited by Edward Connery Lathem. Copyright 1928, 1969 by Henry Holt and Company, Inc., renewed © 1956 by Robert Frost. Used with permission.

"A Song in the Front Yard" from *Selected Poems* by Gwendolyn Brooks, published by HarperCollins. Copyright © 1963 by Gwendolyn Brooks. All rights reserved. Used by permission of the Estate of Gwendolyn Brooks.

"Disillusionment of Ten O'Clock" and "Of Mere Being" from *The Collected Poems of Wallace Stevens*, published by Vintage Books, a division of Random House, Inc. Copyright © 1990 by Random House, In. All rights reserved. Used with permission.

"Another April" from Collected Poems by *James Merrill*, published by Alfred A. Knopf, a division of Random House, Inc. Copyright © 2001 by Alfred A Knopf. All rights reserved. Used with permisssion.

"The House" from *Mysticism for Beginners* by Adam Zagajewski and translated from the Polish by Clare Cavanagh, published by Farrar, Straus, and Giroux. Copyright © 1998 by Farrar, Straus, and Giroux. All rights reserved. Used with permission.

"What the Dog Perhaps Hears" from *Alive Together: New and Selected Poems* by Lisel Mueller, published by Louisiana State University Press. Copyright © 1996 by Louisiana State University Press. Used with permission of Louisiana State University Press.

"Nest" from *Poems: New and Selected* by Marianne Boruch, published by Oberlin College Press. Copyright © 2004 by Oberlin College Press. Used by permission of the author.

FRIENDS & GHOSTS

"Animals" from *Collected Poems* by Frank O'Hara. Copyright © 1971 by Maureen Granville-Smith, Administratrix of the Estate of Frank O'Hara. Used with permission.

"Letter" from *New Selected Poems* by Mark Strand, published by Alfred A. Knopf, a division of Random House, Inc. Copyright © 2007 by Alfred A. Knopf, a division of Random House, Inc. All rights reserved. Used by permission of the author.

"Sadie and Maud" from *Selected Poems* by Gwendolyn Brooks, published by HarperCollins. Copyright © 1963 by Gwendolyn Brooks. All rights reserved. Used by permission of the Estate of Gwendolyn Brooks.

"Margaret and Dusty" from *Grave of Light: New and Selected Poems: 1970-2005* by Alice Notley, published by Wesleyan University Press. Copyright © 2007 by Wesleyan University Press. All rights reserved. Used with permission.

"The Reassurance" and "My Sad Captains" from *Collected Poems by Thom Gunn*, published by Farrar, Straus, and Giroux. Copyright © 2005 by Farrar, Straus, and Giroux. All rights reserved. Used with permission.

"Consider a Move" from *New and Selected Poems* by Michael Ryan, published by Houghton Mifflin. Copyright © 2004 by Houghton Mifflin. All rights reserved. Used by permission of the author.

"Bees" from *Door in the Mountain: New and Collected Poems, 1965-2003* by Jean Valentine, published by Wesleyan University Press. Copyright © 2004 by Wesleyan University Press. All rights reserved. Used with permission.

"The Wound" from *Simplicity* by Ruth Stone, published by Paris Press. Copyright © 1995 by Paris Press. All rights reserved. Used with permission.

"That Sure is My Little Dog" from *Our Post-Soviet History Unfolds* by Eleanor Lerman, published by Sarabande Books. Copyright © 2005 by Sarabande Books. All rights reserved. Used by permission of the author.

"White Dog" from *The Rest of Love* by Carl Phillips, published by Farrar, Straus, and Giroux. Copyright © 2004 by Farrar, Straus, and Giroux. All rights reserved. Used by permission of the author.

"Definition of Stranger" from *The Next Country* by Idra Novey, published by Alice James Books. Copyright © 2008 by Alice James Books. All rights reserved. Used by permission of the author.

"People Getting Divorced" from *Endless Life: Selected Poems* by Lawrence Ferlinghetti, published by New Directions Publishing Corporation. Copyright © 1976 by New Directions Publishing Corporation. All rights reserved. Used with permission.

"Song" from *Fire Lyric* by Cynthia Zarin, published by Alfred A. Knopf, a division of Random House, Inc. Copyright © 1993 by Alfred A. Knopf, a division of Random House, Inc. All rights reserved. Used with permission.

"Poem" from *Rise Up* by Matthew Rohrer, published by Wave Books. Copyright © 2007 by Wave Books. All rights reserved. Used with permission.

"The Shampoo" from *The Complete Poems: 1927-1979* by Elizabeth Bishop, published by Farrar, Straus, and Giroux. Copyright © 1984 by Farrar, Straus, and Giroux. All rights reserved. Used with permission.

"Man of War" by Carol Frost. Copyright © 2008 by Carol Frost. All rights reserved. Used by permission of the author.

"Winter" from *Springing: New and Selected Poems* by Marie Ponsot, published by Alfred A. Knopf, a division of Random House, Inc. Copyright © 2003 by Alfred A. Knopf, a division of Random House, Inc. All rights reserved. Used with permission.

"The Underworld" from *Crown of Weeds* by Amy Gerstler, published by Penguin Books. Copyright © 1997 by Penguin Books. All rights reserved. Used by permission of the author and Penguin Group (USA), Inc.

MYSELF I SPEAK & SPELL

"Olympia" from *Middle Earth* by Henri Cole, published by published by Farrar, Straus, and Giroux. Copyright © 2004 by Farrar, Straus, and Giroux. All rights reserved. Used with permission.

"Tenderness and Rot" from *The Niagara River* by Kay Ryan, published by Grove Press. Copyright © 2005 by Grove Press. All rights reserved. Used with permission.

"Warning" by Taha Muhammad Ali, translated by Peter Cole from *So What: New and Selected Poems 1973-2005*, published by Copper Canyon Press. Copyright © 2006 by Copper Canyon Press. All rights reserved. Used with permission.

"The Bearhug" from *To a Fault* by Nick Laird, published by W.W. Norton & Company. Copyright © 2006 by W.W. Norton & Company. All rights reserved. Used by permission of the author.

"Samurai Song" from *Jersey Rain* by Robert Pinsky, published by Farrar, Straus, and Giroux. Copyright © 2001 by Farrar, Straus, and Giroux. All rights reserved. Used by permission of the author.

"An Old Cracked Tune" from *The Collected Poems* by Stanley Kunitz, published by W.W. Norton & Company. Copyright © 2002 by W.W. Norton & Company. All rights reserved. Used with permission.

"Remora" from *Collected Poems* by James Merrill, published by Alfred A. Knopf, a division of Random House, Inc. Copyright © 2001 by Alfred A Knopf. All rights reserved. Used with permission.

"Hula" from *New and Selected Poems 1963-1992* by Ron Padgett, published by David R. Godine. Copyright © 1995 by David R. Godine. All rights reserved. Used by permission of the author.

"Mr. T—" from *Hip Logic* by Terrance Hayes, published by Penguin Group (USA), Inc. Copyright © 2002 by Penguin Group (USA), Inc. All rights reserved. Used by permission of the author and Penguin Group (USA), Inc.

"Fame: My Version" from *Filibuster to Delay A Kiss* by Courtney Queeney, published by Alfred A. Knopf, a division of Random House, Inc. Copyright © 2007 by Alfred A Knopf. All rights reserved. Used by permission of the author.

"What Bee Did" by Julie Larios. Copyright © 2006 by Julie Larios. All rights reserved. Used by permission of the author.

"Wiring Home" from *Mother Love* by Rita Dove, published by W.W. Norton & Company. Copyright © 1995 by Rita Dove.

"The wind stopped for a moment" from *Who Whispered Near Me* by Killarney Clary, published by Farrar, Straus, and Giroux. Copyright © 1990 by Farrar, Straus & Giroux. All rights reserved. Used by permission of the author.

"Dusk" from *Veil: New and Selected Poems* by Rae Armantrout, published by Wesleyan University Press. Copyright © 2001 by Wesleyan University Press. All rights reserved. Used with permission of the author.

"Wind in a Box" from *Wind in a Box* by Terrance Hayes, published by Penguin Group (USA), Inc. Copyright © 2006 by Penguin Group (USA), Inc. All rights reserved. Used by permission of the author and Penguin Group (USA), Inc.

"We Are Only Human" from *Elegy* by Mary Jo Bang, published by Graywolf Press. Copyright © 2007 by Graywolf Press. All rights reserved. Used with permission.

"One is One" from *Springing: New and Selected Poems* by Marie Ponsot, published by Alfred A. Knopf, a division of Random House, Inc. Copyright © 2003 by Alfred A Knopf. All rights reserved. Used with permission.

SPRING & AFTER

"The Trees" from *Collected Poems* by Philip Larkin, published by Farrar, Straus, and Giroux. Copyright © 2004 by Farrar, Straus, and Giroux. All rights reserved. Used with permission.

"When Ecstasy is Inconvenient" from *Lorine Niedecker, Collected Works* by Lorine Niedecker, published by University of California Press. Copyright © 2002 by University of California Press. All rights reserved. Used with permission.

"At the End of Summer" from *Ripple Effect: New and Selected Poems* by Elaine Equi, published by Coffee House Press. Copyright © 2007 by Coffee House Press. All rights reserved. Used by permission of the author.

"So I Will Till the Ground" from *So I Will Till the Ground* by Gregory Djanikian, published by Carnegie Mellon University Press. Copyright © 2007 by Carnegie Mellon University Press. All rights reserved. Used by permission of the author.

"The Seasons" from *Columbarium* by Susan Stewart, published by University of Chicago Press. © 2003 by University of Chicago Press. All rights reserved. Used by permission of the author.

"September, Inverness" from *Time and Materials: Poems 1997-2005* by Robert Hass, published by Ecco/HarperCollins. Copyright © 2008 by Ecco / HarperCollins. All rights reserved. Used with permission.

"We Have the Right to Love Autumn" from *Unfortunately, It Was Paradise: Selected Poems* by Mahmoud Darwish, translated from the Arabic by Munir Akash and Carolyn Forché, published by University of California Press. Copyright © 2003 by Regents of the University of California. All rights reserved. Used with permission.

"How lonely it is" from *Haiku: This Other World* by Richard Wright, published by Arcade Publishing.

Copyright © 1998 by Arcade Publishing. All rights reserved. Used with permission.

"Bloom" from *Radio Crackling, Radio Gone* by Lisa Olstein, published by Copper Canyon Press. Copyright © 2006 by Copper Canyon Press. All rights reserved. Used by permission of the author.

"Wintry Mix" from *The Outernationale* by Peter Gizzi, published by Wesleyan University Press. Copyright © 2007 by Wesleyan University Press. All rights reserved. Used by permission of the author.

"December" from *New and Selected Poems 1963-1992* by Ron Padgett, published by David R. Godine. Copyright © 1995 by David R. Godine. All rights reserved. Used by permission of the author.

"The Day of Cold Food" from *One Hundred Poems from the Chinese* by Li Chi'ng Chao, translated by Kenneth Rexroth, published by New Directions Publishing Corporation. Copyright © 1971 by New Directions Publishing Corporation. All rights reserved. Used with permission.

"Aubade" from *They Are Sleeping* by Joanna Klink, published by University of Georgia Press. Copyright © 2000 by University of Georgia Press. All rights reserved. Used by permission of the author.

CITY, MY CITY

From "The Invention of Streetlights" in *Goest* by Cole Swensen, published by Alice James Books. Copyright © 2004 by Alice James Books. All rights reserved. Used by permission of the author.

"Side 19," and "Side 32" from *Maraca: New and Selected Poems 1965-2000* by Victor Hernández Cruz, published by Coffee House Press. © 2001 by Coffee House Press. All rights reserved. Used by permission of the author.

From "The City in Which I Love You" in *The City in Which I Love You* by Li-Young Lee, published by BOA Editions, Ltd. Copyright © 1990 by BOA Editions, Ltd. Used with permission.

"Henry hates the world" (#74) from *The Dream Songs* by John Berryman, published by Farrar, Straus, and Giroux. Copyright © 1969 by Farrar, Straus, and Giroux. All rights reserved. Used with permission.

"100 Riverside: Waking Up at Mari's" from *The Displaced of Capital* by Anne Winters, published by the University of Chicago Press. Copyright © 2004 by University of Chicago Press. All rights reserved. Used by permission of the author.

"O Woolly City" from *O Woolly City* by Priscilla Sneff, published by Tupelo Press. Copyright © 2007 by Tupelo Press. Used by permission of Tupelo Press.

"Broken Sonnet" from *Paradiso Diaspora* by John Yau, published by Penguin Books. Copyright © 2006 by Penguin Books. Used by permission of the author.

"In Antigua" from *We Do Not Eat Our Hearts Alone* by Kerri Webster, published by University of Georgia Press. Copyright © 2005 by University of Georgia Press. All rights reserved. Used by permission of the author.

"The Hungarian Pastry Shop & Café" from *Floating City* by Anne Pierson Wiese, published by Louisiana State University Press. Copyright © 2008 by Louisiana State University Press. Used by permission of the author and LSU Press.

"Catwalk" from *Talking Dirty to the Gods* by Yusef Komunyakaa, published by Farrar, Straus, and Giroux. Copyright © 2001 by Farrar, Straus, and Giroux. All rights reserved. Used by permission of the author.

"Fear" from *Begin Again: Collected Poems* by Grace Paley, published by Farrar, Straus, and Giroux. Copyright © 2000 by Farrar, Straus, and Giroux. All rights reserved. Used with permission.

"Coyotes in Greenwich!" from *Orient Point* by Julie Sheehan, published by W.W. Norton & Company. Copyright 2007 by W.W. Norton & Company. All rights reserved. Used by permission of the author.

"DSS Dream" from *City of Coughing and Dead Radiators* by Martín Espada, published by W.W. Norton & Company. Copyright 1994 by W.W. Norton & Company. All rights reserved. Used by permission of the author.

"Harm" from *Collected Poems* by C.K. Williams, published by Farrar, Straus, and Giroux. Copyright © 2006 by Farrar, Straus, and Giroux. All rights reserved. Used with permission.

"Meat" from *Sleeping it Off in Rapid City: Poems, New and Selected* by August Kleinzahler, published by Farrar, Straus, and Giroux. Copyright © 2008 by Farrar, Straus, and Giroux. All rights reserved. Used with permission.

"Shark's Teeth" from *The Niagara River* by Kay Ryan, published by Grove Press. Copyright © 2005 by Grove Press. All rights reserved. Used with permission.

"Transcontinent" from *Old and New Poems* by Donald Hall, published by Houghton Mifflin. Copyright © 1990 by Houghton Mifflin. Used with permission.

EATING & DRINKING

"cutting greens" by Lucille Clifton from *An Ordinary Woman*, published by Random House, Inc. Copyright © 1974 by Lucille Clifton. Used with permission.

"All the Soups" from *At the Gate by Martha Rhodes*, published by Provincetown Arts Press. Copyright © 1995 by Provincetown Arts Press. Used with permission.

"Honey" by Arielle Greenberg. Copyright 2008 © by Arielle Greenberg. All rights reserved. Used by permission of the author.

"Self-Portrait as a Bear" from *White Apples and the Taste of Stone: Selected Poems 1946-2006* by Donald Hall, published by Houghton Mifflin. Copyright © 2006 by Houghton Mifflin. All rights reserved. Used with permission.

"Lost in the Forest" from *Nerve Storm* by Amy Gerstler, published by Penguin Books. Copyright © 1993 by Penguin Books. All rights reserved. Used with permission.

"Kitchen Song" from *Dance and Disappear* by Laura Kasischke, published by University of Massachusetts Press. Copyright © 2002 by University of Massachusetts Press. Used by permission of the author.

"Freezer" from *Hunger* by Lola Haskins, published by University of Iowa Press. Copyright © 1993 by University of Iowa Press. Used by permission of the author.

"Red Beans" from *Maraca: New and Selected Poems 1965-2000* by Victor Hernández Cruz, published by Coffee House Press. © 2001 by Coffee House Press. All rights reserved. Used by permission of the author.

"Avocado" from *Turtle Island* by Gary Snyder, published by New Directions Publishing Corporation. Copyright © 1969 by New Directions Publishing Corporation. Used with permission.

"Watermelons" from *Return to a Place Lit By a Glass of Milk* by Charles Simic, published by George Braziller. Copyright © 1974 by Charles Simic. Used with permission.

"Spaghetti" by Gerald Stern. Copyright © 2008 by Gerald Stern. All rights reserved. Used by permission of the author.

From "Leap" in *Rain* by Jon Woodward, published by Wave Books. Copyright © 2006 by Wave Books. Used by permission of the author.

"The Thirties" from *Mysticism for Beginners* by Adam Zagajewski and translated from the Polish by Clare Cavanagh, published by Farrar, Straus, and Giroux. Copyright © 1998 by Farrar, Straus, and Giroux. All rights reserved. Used with permission.

"Tomato" from *Antebellum Dream Book* by Elizabeth Alexander, published by Graywolf Press. Copyright © 2001 by Graywolf Press. All rights reserved. Used with permission.

"Styrofoam Cup" from *Cascadia* by Brenda Hillman, published by Wesleyan University Press. Copyright © 2001 by Wesleyan University Press. All rights reserved. Used with permission of the author.

"A Glass of Water" from *Collected Poems: 1930-1993* by May Sarton, published by W.W. Norton & Company. Copyright 1982 by W.W. Norton & Company. All rights reserved. Used with permission.

"Going Off the Deep End Into Confectionery" from *Sad Little Breathing Machine* by Matthea Harvey, published by Graywolf Press. Copyright © 2004 by Graywolf Press. All rights reserved. Used with permission.

"Ciao Bella Chocolate Sorbet" from *Ripple Effect: New and Selected Poems* by Elaine Equi, published by Coffee House Press. Copyright © 2007 by Coffee House Press. Used by permission of the author.

SONIC YOUTH

"Into the Land of Youth" from *Potential Stranger* by Killarney Clary, published by University of Chicago Press. Copyright © 2003 by University of Chicago Press. All rights reserved. Used by permission of the author.

From "Games with Children" in *Red Rover* by Susan Stewart, published by University of Chicago Press. Copyright © 2008 by University of Chicago Press. All rights reserved. Used by permission of the author.

"By Daylight" from *A Woman Kneeling in the Big City* by Elizabeth Macklin, published by W. W. Norton & Company, Copyright © 1992 by W.W. Norton & Company. All rights reserved. Used with permission.

"The Old Man and the Motorcycle" from *The Executive Director of the Fallen World* by Liam Rector, published by University of Chicago Press, Copyright © 2006 by University of Chicago Press. All rights reserved. Used with permission.

"Muzak" from *Jelly Roll* by Kevin Young, published by Alfred A. Knopf, a division of Random House, Inc. Copyright © 2003 by Alfred A Knopf. All rights reserved. Used with permission.

"Weather" from *Skies* by Eileen Myles, published by Black Sparrow Press. Copyright © 2001 by Eileen Myles. All rights reserved. Used by permission of the author.

"Flood Plain" from *Primitive Mentor* by Dean Young, published by University of Pittsburgh Press. Copyright © 2008 by University of Pittsburgh Press. All rights reserved. Used by permission of the author.

"The Lighthouse Keeper" from *Halflife* by Meghan O'Rourke, published by W.W. Norton & Company. Copyright © 2008 by W.W. Norton & Company. All rights reserved. Used with permission.

"I Go Back to May, 1937" from *The Gold Cell* by Sharon Olds, published by Alfred A. Knopf, a division of Random House, Inc. Copyright © 1987 by Alfred A. Knopf, a division of Random House, Inc. All rights reserved. Used with permission.

"Winter Field" from *Shadow of Heaven* by Ellen Bryant Voigt, published by W.W. Norton & Company. Copyright © 2002 by W.W. Norton & Company. All rights reserved. Used with permission.

"Lament for the Makers" from *In the Western Night: Collected Poems 1965-1990* by Frank Bidart, published by Farrar, Straus, and Giroux. Copyright © 2000 by Farrar, Straus, and Giroux. All rights reserved. Used with permission.

"From My Father's Side of the Bed" from *What the Living Do* by Marie Howe, published by W.W. Norton & Company. Copyright © 1998 by W.W. Norton & Company. All rights reserved. Used with permission.

"The Man Splitting Wood in the Daybreak" from *Three Books* by Galway Kinnell, published by Houghton Mifflin. Copyright © 2002 by Houghton Mifflin. All rights reserved. Used by permission of the author.

"There is Never Enough Time" from *A Book of Witness* by Jerome Rothenberg, published by New Directions. Copyright © 2002 by Jerome Rothenberg. All rights reserved. Used by permission of the author.

"After Reading Tu Fu, I Go Outside to the Dwarf Orchard" from *Chickamauga* by Charles Wright, published by Farrar, Straus, and Giroux. Copyright © 1995 by Farrar, Straus, and Giroux. All rights reserved. Used by permission of the author.

"Six Apologies, Lord" from *shattered sonnets love cards and other off and back handed importunities* by Olena Kalytiak Davis, published by Bloomsbury/Tin House. Copyright © 2003 by Bloomsbury/Tin House. All rights reserved. Used with permission.

"Erotic Energy" from *The Snow Watcher* by Chase Twichell, published by Ontario Review Press. Copyright © 1998 by Chase Twichell. All rights reserved. Used by permission of the author.

"The Red Poppy" from *The Wild Iris* by Louise Glück, published by HarperCollins Publishers. Copyright © 1992 by HarperCollins Publishers. All rights reserved. Used with permission.